Introducing AUSTRALIA

WRITTEN, PHOTOGRAPHED
AND DESIGNED BY
GORDON DE'LISLE
FRPS, FRSA, EFIAP.

ADDITIONAL PHOTOGRAPHY,
RESEARCH AND CO-ORDINATION BY
CYNTHIA DE'LISLE

JOEY BOOKS
MELBOURNE

First published 1969
by Joey Books Pty. Ltd.,
81-83 City Road, South Melbourne,
Victoria, Australia 3205.
GORDON DE'LISLE
Managing Editor.

Printed in the British Crown
Colony of Hong Kong
by
Toppan Printing Company (H.K.) Ltd.

NATIONAL LIBRARY OF AUSTRALIA
REGISTRY NUMBER Aus 68-4295.

Text set in Monotype, Plantin 10 on 12 point,
by Dudley E. King Pty. Ltd., Melbourne.

Introducing AUSTRALIA

For our children
Jennie, Chris, Jamie
and Rodney,
who make our house a home
and keep us young.

Acknowledgements

SPECIAL THANKS are due to Ray Harber, Managing Editor of *Australia Today*, who made our wanderings possible. His Associate Editor, Dick Williams, sub-edited the literary content of this book with true understanding of its purpose, and with patient concern. Clive Turnbull and John Brennan gave me counsel and encouragement. The Commonwealth Department of Trade and Industry helped me with maps and valuable advice, and the statistics were re-written from those supplied by the Commonwealth Bureau of Census and Statistics. The end-paper maps are reproduced by courtesy of The Swire Group. Personal thanks are due to the hundreds of Australians who gave my wife and myself shelter, comfort and unstinting help.

G.D.

CONTENTS

Introduction

THE MATERIAL IN THIS BOOK expresses the feelings and opinions of the writer, with some exceptions. These are the hotel and restaurant ratings, in Chapter 2, 'Of Statistics and Cities'. It was felt that the opinions of one, or two, could legitimately be described as unfair. Therefore, twenty-four people were polled as to their preferences. They included journalists, a TV interviewer, travel managers of two airlines, one restaurateur, a hotel chain manager (who didn't mention a single one of his own houses), two management consultants, two American directors, two dear old ladies who travel on buses, one chronic epicurean knocker, and the managing director of Australia's finest winery. The results are as shown. But please be it understood that the restaurants and hotels we have rated are not all (there are probably another hundred fine restaurants in Melbourne, and an equal number in Sydney); they simply reflect the preferences of the writer and of 24 of his acquaintances. Places were excluded because they didn't give value for money, because they were grubby, because their staff in public contact were insolent; or simply because 24 very well-travelled Australians didn't know they exist. The rated list probably will be expanded in our next edition.

CHAPTER 1

AN EMERGENT IDENTITY

THIS PARADOX continent, Australia, is an emptiness fringed with gardens—desiccated land rimmed by emerald.

From rain-jungles impenetrable to the burliest bull-dozer, to deserts treeless for a hundred miles—Australia could look like home to almost any soul on Earth.

Australia is seasonless—somewhere there is always sun. While hawk-faced skiers schuss efflorescent alpine slopes, farmers athwart the Tropic of Capricorn tend sugar-cane, susurrous-stirred in the dreaming warmth of valleys, counties-long.

This greatest of islands is populated by not nearly enough amiable, paradoxical sun-lovers who have never known famine, pestilence, subjection, or broad-scale civil commotion; yet they are Indian and Pacific Ocean bed-fellows of awakening Asian giants to whom calamities are concomitants of daily life.

Four-fifths of all Australians live in cities and, like all city-dwellers, are totally involved in the business of playing, working, procreating; sating their appetites and quelling their concerns. One-fifth of Australia's people live in the country or the outback—and it is this fifth who are in touch with Australia's beating heart, as close to the essence of the land as anyone on earth.

To their grievous disappointment, Australians are not well-known to the world at large . . . just why this should be a source of disappointment they can't tell. True, Australian swimmers, golfers and tennists are known in the United States; Australian cricketers, rugby players, tourists and actors are known in England; Australian singers are known in Italy, and Australian painters are known in Paris. But by-and-large the image in the mind's-eye of most of the world's people is of koalas and kangaroos, wide hats, beer, racehorses, incomprehensible speech, censorship, cultural mediocrity . . . and a near-total disinterest in the affairs of civilized living.

Much of this image was created in the fool's-paradise past, when Australia, unemergent and somnolent, complacent behind the guns of Singapore and white-ensigned might, had settled down to the balmy prospect of a century of lounging in a sun-filled vacuum.

World War II changed this quickly, absolutely and permanently. Australia was rammed on shaky feet out of the amniotic fluid of Empire into responsible adulthood.

The old sweet days of somnolence will never return, because Australia now must move; not only as fast as the world about her, but preferably much, much faster.

World War was a shock, and although barely touched directly, Australia, with one of the world's highest enlistment rates, watched the cream of her youth board transports heading for alien death.

Australians fought in the Battle of Britain, in the Western Desert, at Singapore and on the deeps of the Atlantic Approaches. They flew Spitfires out of Malta, manned tramps to Murmansk and went barge-busting in Burma.

Men who queued to enlist in Australia in the first week of September 1939, had fought through a score of countries and found themselves slushing waist-deep through Pacific Island swamps when peace arrived six weary years later.

The War's cost to Australia was in all ways enormous, but the side-effects were invaluable.

The world had seen Australians at their profane, able, cheerful best . . . and Australians had seen the world at its cruellest, dreariest worst.

The Australians returned, at least one to every average family, with the certain knowledge that never again could their continent drowse . . . the war was over, but the turmoil only beginning.

Australia took global stock of her situation.

Post-war aircraft had shrunk the world by half, and jets were about to halve it again.

Ninety million Indonesians stood emergent and demanding, soon to be minutes flying-time from mainland Australia, soon also to share a common border with Australian New Guinea.

". . . never again could the continent drowse." ⟩
Australians reach for the clouds with new buildings.
These are Sydney's Australia Square towers. Summit
Restaurant forms round-tower's tiara.

All of Asia was stirring and flexing: a thousand million people now stood athwart the tenuous lines to the Mother Country, herself sorely beset internally.

Australia's path stood clear, and men of vision, heedful of the winds of change, set her firmly on it. Though grappling with enormous problems of reconversion for peace, and rehabilitation for the servicemen, a policy of intense immigration stood uppermost.

"Populate or Perish" became a grimly true slogan of the day.

And so the migrants came . . . poets and painters, welders and waiters, doctors and dancers, barbers and butchers, scientists and shipbuilders—the trickle became a flood and the flood became a torrent. A new excitement possessed the land, and the miracle of Australia in the 1960's came into being.

Australia had to recover from the war, house natural growth, open its gates to migrant millions, pay their passage ten thousand miles, teach them and their children a new language and way of life, and give each one of them the opportunity to make a living, build a home . . . and become an Australian.

What in retrospect could have been a disastrous gamble paid off, many-fold. Australia coped, and grew—and is growing fast.

But the greater part of the miracle, like an iceberg, is below the surface.

Sceptics had said that old Australians, steeped in insularity and suspicion of things alien, would never accept these "New Australians". Instead, acceptance was immediate, complete and intense.

Australians were happy to extend the hand of welcome, and New Australians were happy to grasp it. Near-total assimilation has been one of the great successes of the immigration program.

Now there are so many New Australian mayors of communities, champion sportsmen and sportswomen, and executives of big business that the novelty has palled; strange names no longer excite comment or hold significance.

A surprising feature of the kind of spectacular immigration going on to Australia has been the lack of any corresponding rise in cultural levels. The values that have changed most are those of

"And so the migrants came . . . the trickle became a flood and the flood became a torrent." **German girl, her most treasured possession a rag doll, faces her future as a** *"New Australian".*

the migrants; they seem to find home and garden and friendly neighbours more rewarding than perhaps they did at home, and their hunger for cultural pursuits is amply gratified by these simple rewards for their toil. And what assimilative aid has been forthcoming from the children . . . who on Australian earth could resist a cheerful grin of a tiny Italian face impishly sucking an icecream, or the phrase "Oweryergoin' mate . . . orright?" issuing from a crew-cropped little Latvian?

Today the scale of migration remains enormous (one in five of Australians were not born here), and the Australian government's dedication to the value of migrants remains unchanged, no matter which party is in power.

If Australia can't find enough ships to bring out her new people, she charters jets and flies whole families across a world at the cost to them of a weekend jaunt.

So they come . . . and so Australia grows.

Mines and smelters rear their towers with crash-program urgency; "beef" roads spider-web their way across areas dun-colored "arid" on quickly obsolescent maps; great pumps finger their way through eons-old shale to tap artesian seas and oil pools; and power shovels, as massive as apartment houses, tear the tops from mountains made of iron.

Builders'-labourers in Melbourne ballot for land, shelve their tools, and caravan with wives and children to opposite ends of the continent to try the gamble of rural life, perhaps an hour's jet-flight from Indonesian soil.

Oil gouts green from Australian earth, flocks grow bigger, grain grows higher, factories pour out abundance . . . and hopes are boundless.

All a man needs in the new Australia is ambition and energy, and he can be a towering giant.

Australia's future is as limitless as her horizons and the hearts of Australians.

"Mines and smelters rear their towers with crash-program urgency . . ." **Giant mobile conveyer stock-piles Australian iron ore for export at new port of Dampier, near Port Hedland, NW Western Australia.**

CHAPTER 2

OF STATISTICS AND CITIES

T HINK THE Australian's a hayseed? Or that Australia's a desert of hick towns and kangaroos?
Forget it!

The Australian is urban, perceptive, sharp in business and sophisticated in knowledge. He's in the world forefront of virus research and radio astronomy; he builds supersonic jet aircraft, high-performance automobiles which he exports to 71 countries, and simply dandy computers.

He grows extraordinary crosses of high-yield wheat, breeds the world's best merino sheep . . . and new cattle crosses, staggering steak bearers "the size of locomotives."

He lives on about three million square miles of land which, averaged, is the most arid on earth. Australia holds in its heart the world's 3rd, 8th, 9th, 12th and 17th largest deserts (some of them not seeing a rainspot for ten years), yet it is blessed with a coastal strip thousands of miles long that in places luxuriates in rainfalls of 180 *inches!* Oh, yes . . . there are also Alps, with snowfields many times bigger in area than Switzerland.

Highest temperature, a searing 125° in the shade; lowest temperature, *eight!*

Australia's three million square miles are roughly the size of the mainland United States, or ten times that of Austria, 250 times Belgium, 24 times France, 21 times the two Germanys, 60 times Greece, 27 times Italy, 240 times The Netherlands, 32 times the United Kingdom . . . or 21 times Japan.

But, chilling fact, Australia's population is only the same as London's; and world densities of population to the square mile are Japan 660, Europe-U.K. 230, South Asia 300, South-East Asia 135, East Asia 200, North America 26, USSR 26 . . . Australia, *four!*

"... the most arid country on earth, yet blessed with a coastal strip thousands of miles long that in places luxuriates in rainfalls of 180 inches!" **Sugar at Queensland's Proserpine; horizon is Barrier Reef.**

Of Australia's 12 millions, 900,000 were born in the United Kingdom and Ireland, 267,000 in Italy, 110,000 in Germany, 100,000 in Poland, 140,000 in Greece, and 55,000 in Malta.

Australia's 12 million (including 8½ million Protestants and 3 million Catholics) graze 170 *million* sheep, and farm 40 million acres of land from which they crop 470 million bushels of wheat, 200 million bushels of oats, barley and other cereals . . . and 17 million tons of sugar-cane.

From the miserable, cruel mining country Australians tear annually one million ounces of gold, 375,000 tons of lead, 100,000 tons of copper, 400,000 tons of zinc, and 60 *million* tons of coal. Australia produced no bauxite for aluminium in 1945, a bit in the 1950's . . . but 3 *million* tons in 1968. Australia produced 2 million tons of iron ore in 1945 . . . but in 1969 one company, Hamersley, not the biggest, exported 17 *million* tons. There is concern over the fact that 100 foreign companies, half of them American, now prospect for Australian minerals.

To export—yet still eat better than anyone else on earth (including 12 ounces of meat and fish a day, 50 per cent more than the U.S.A. and U.K., 5 times Japan, 30 times India)— Australians annually produce 1,500 *million* gallons of milk, kill 3 million pigs, graze 20 million cattle, grow 12 million bushels of oranges and make 34 million gallons of ice-cream. Their food bill is 3¼ *thousand million dollars*. For their delightful potables they harvest 1,500 tons of dried hops which they amiably brew into 350 million gallons of beer; and crop a third of a million tons of wine grapes.

Seventy-five per cent of Australians crowd into the cities, occupying two per cent of the land. From 63,000 factories employing one and a third million workers they pour out 16,000 *million* dollars' worth of goods, including 350 million dollars of clothing, nearly a thousand million dollars of food, drink and tobacco, 100 million dollars of beds and bedding . . . and to soothe the savage breast, 7 million dollars of musical instruments.

Annually, Australia's 12 millions make 30 million pairs of shoes, make and lay one and a third *thousand-million* bricks which they stick together with nearly four million tons of local

". . . the miserable, cruel mining country . . ."
Australians at Hamersley Iron tear the top from
Mount Tom Price, on the edge of Western Australia's
Great Sandy Desert. 120 degrees in the shade is
commonplace.

cement . . . and weave 25 million square yards of cloth. They turn out 3 million electric motors, 650 million lbs. of golden canned fruit, 80 million pairs of stockings and panty-hose, 6 million tons of steel and 100,000 tons of newsprint.

They keep their houses gay with 16 million gallons of paint; and their beer cool with the production each year of a quarter of a million refrigerators.

They complete about 2 *thousand million* dollars' worth of buildings each year; but one Australian in four works for government.

In 1964–65 the Gross National Product was $A19,852 million; in 1967–68 it was $A24,214 million.

Australia's 12 millions drive 4½ million motor vehicles, on which they spend 800 million dollars annually (one family in three drives more than one car); they are haunted by three and one-third million telephones . . . and they squat semi-comatose, bemused, benumbed and besotted before 2½ million television screens; when not listening to eleven million radio sets.

As behooves the most air-minded people on earth, 5 million passenger tickets are issued domestically, for 58 million miles of flying. A thousand-mile trip to see a promising horse or a more promising lady is not uncommon; and Australia's overseas services carry half a million passengers 30 million miles.

Australia's 12 million have 12 *thousand million* dollars socked away in the bank, and 2½ thousand million with life insurance companies . . . but they owe finance companies 1½ thousand million dollars, which perhaps helps explain the purchase of 87 million dollars' worth of hope, in the form of lottery tickets.

Gambling Australians annually make 700 million half-dollar bets on horses and dogs through totalisators, and fatten bookies' bags to the tune of 655 million dollars.

Ninety-six thousand marriages between eager, nubile young Australians are consummated each year . . . but nearly one in ten ends in tears, recriminations and divorce courts. 223,000 babies are born annually to Australian mothers, but a surprising number of these appearances come to pass from unsanctified unions, and an even more surprising number from unions

The affluent Australians, *"with 12 thousand million dollars socked away in the bank. . . ."* Elegant, handsome young people enjoy champagne racing and champagne picnic at Melbourne's Derby Day, during spring carnival.

sanctified in the nick of time. This probably has some correlation with the balmy climate.

Each year 105,000 Australians go to meet their maker; 30,000 from heart trouble, 16,000 from cancer, and 14,000 from cerebral haemorrhage . . . but more than 3,000 die horribly and wastefully in shattered cars; and 1,700, seeing no way out, end it all by their own hand.

115,000 immigrants seek a bright future each year, but one in ten finds the break too much, and goes home.

18,000 policemen help 12 million Australians along the paths of righteousness, but 7,500 Australians are currently undertaking correction in penal establishments for having strayed.

Australia welcomes half a million visitors each year.

Specifically for visitors, committed or intending, here is a pen-picture, necessarily superficial, of the cities which will be their landfall or homes as they arrive in search of instruction, pleasure . . . or work.

It can also be read with advantage by Australians who think they know their home cities. It is the result not only of personal perception, but also of having answered many thorny questions from fellow ship and air passengers, and from business visitors and tourists and their ladies. It is the result also of having later shared their opinions.

Captioning a couple of hundred thousand photographs of these cities has helped.

SYDNEY, *population 2½ million, capital of the State of New South Wales, population 4½ million.*

Breathtakingly bustling, bigger than Rome, Sydney is sited around a superb harbour that rivals Rio's, and functions as focal point of much of its industry, recreation and way of life. Things big get done, fast (excepting the Opera House, a challenge that went sour).

A gay, exciting city, with a score of excellent hotels and a hundred Lucullan restaurants; where you can enjoy char Angus steaks as big as briefcases, sukiyaki, nasi goreng, exceptional

"... sited around a superb harbour that rivals Rio's."
**Bustling ferries and super-liner Canberra in Sydney
Cove. Bridge links "North-Shore" half of Sydney with
city proper, carries fantastic traffic densities.**

seafood, a hundred curries, toheroa and kangaroo-tail soups, Peking duck, bouillabaisse, prosciutto ham and melon—or your fancy from four-page French menus traditionally handwritten in purple ink, Italian menus without prices, broadsheet-sized; or German menus borne by mini-skirted Bavarian hostesses.

You can also buy, for cents, a hero hamburger made from the identical ground lean beef that Californians import for their *best* hamburgers.

Wash these good things down with ambrosial libations . . . the wines of the Hunter Valley, a hundred miles to the north.

Sydney shows movies before New York, has excellent live theatre (particularly the 'little' theatres), but poor facilities for symphony. It is Australia's jazz centre.

The art gallery has excellent Australian art, very poorly shown because of appalling facilities.

Sydney is Australia's centre for forbidden delights, which it tolerates realistically—your taxi-driver or bell-captain is access to things improper, yet conducted with *élan* and a certain flourish.

The city's doings are reported by two excellent morning newspapers, a tabloid and a broadsheet, which also report the world in responsible fashion. The two evening dailies, which make first appearances in mid-morning, though responsible, are entertainment newspapers, and posters declaiming SHOCK RAPE QUIZ PROBE! are instantly interpreted by Sydneysiders as referring to something mildly unpleasant that occurred in a remote South American banana republic to an idiot peasant girl.

Sydney is flanked to north and south by blindingly beautiful beaches, well conducted and maintained, and populated by some of the most physically perfect people on earth; lithe, golden girls, straight as arrows, proudly high-breasted, ripe and luscious . . . and brimming with friendly, un-arrogant self-confidence.

Sydney Harbour cuts the city in halves, the City proper and the North Shore . . . and the two halves are linked by the Sydney Harbour Bridge, an antique toll bridge of great character which (although it ranks only about fortieth in the world's list of principal bridges) carries fantastic traffic densities.

"...*flanked to north and south by blindingly beauti-ful beaches....*" Complex of golden sand arcs northward from Manly, rimmed by its celebrated Norfolk Island pines. City is thirty minutes by ferry, fifty by car.

Travel by underground trains; fast, convenient, and well-run. Sydney taxis are actually cunningly disguised army tanks, often driven by individuals sweatshirted and unshaven like bilge-cleaners on Panamanian tramps.

Ferry rides on the harbour, to a score of destinations, are a delight for only a few cents; and one can with profit spend scores of happy hours, with a few chicken sandwiches and a bag of fresh fruit bought on the ferry wharves, puttering around the harbour's nooks and crannies, ferryborne.

14 million people ride Sydney's 41 ferries each year.

Try to become a guest on a yacht or cruiser picnic on Sydney Harbour, any weekend. Carefree people in thousands of craft (including more than 2,000 yachts) enjoy such dream excursions. A very special delight is a beef and burgundy barbecue at, say, Quarantine Bay, one of hundreds indenting the harbour fringe. There will be much boat-to-boat intercourse and water-borne good feeling, and your day will probably culminate in a twilight cruise around the harbourside city and suburbs . . . with a myriad diamond lights shimmering the water, and the bridge a jewelled tiara in the sky.

Enchantment!

Saturdays the harbour plays host to the Eighteen-Footers, a class of yacht, semi-professional, whose tiny squat hulls are crewed by some of the huskiest rascals on earth; manhandling enough sail to make a set of curtains for a good-sized theatre. Take a ride for a few cents on the ferry that accompanies them, but don't be surprised if a police cruiser with the jolly name of 'Nemesis' chooses to board . . . you see, many of your travel companions would prove to be bookies, illegally betting on the races.

Shopping in Sydney is dandy; especially in the little arcade shops or the chic suburbs like Double Bay. Buy woollens (garments or dress and suit lengths), shoes, opals and wines. Don't buy goods made from kangaroo fur . . . you'd be contributing to the mass murder of one of the most enchanting, inoffensive creatures on earth!

Go to King's Cross, a kind of satellite city, which roars all night and where naughty things happen. This is where kooks,

". . . the Eighteen-Footers . . . tiny hulls crewed by some of the huskiest rascals on earth. . . ." **Maritime mayhem as world's biggest sail carriers (for size) clash in roiling seas of Southerly Busters.**

cranks, queers and ladies with ambivalent attitudes to virtue are prone to gather. Gaze at them, but do dress casually, in order that you may be gazed back at and dubbed either kook, crank or queer . . .

Lunch in The Summit restaurant, and you will find yourself in gastronomic orbit, 47 floors in the sky, with the whole of Sydney spread out as an extension of your tablecloth. In the time elapsing between your fresh Prawn Cocktail, through your Carpetbag Steak stuffed with Sydney Rock Oysters, and the culminating Orange Soufflé, you will have made one full revolution, drunk a bottle of good wine, and have a benign rosy-hued knowledge of Sydney perhaps greater than many of its troglodyte flat-dwellers.

Worship at the Wayside Chapel, King's Cross, and St. Mark's, Darling Point, and you'll also know a great deal about Sydney's people.

Sydney's a swinger!

Sydney's social establishment is predicated on what people have achieved.

WHERE TO EAT IN SYDNEY

ARGYLE TAVERN, Argyle Street.
Good food, old colonial decor in the historic "Rocks" area, under the Bridge.

BUONASERA, Macleay Street, King's Cross.
For a delicious "pop-in" Italian meal, unexcelled. Cheap.

CAPRICE, on the Harbour, at Rose Bay.
Elegant, ultimate service. Fine food, gentle music; giant picture windows to the Harbour. Very expensive.

CHELSEA, Macleay Street, King's Cross.
Lush, gracious decor; all crimson and candles. Fine food, discreet service. Very expensive.

"*. . . find yourself in gastronomic orbit, 47 floors in the sky. . . .*" Twilight at the Summit Restaurant, garnished with diamonds, rubies, emeralds . . . and antlike ferries and ships circumnavigating your tablecloth.

CHEQUERS, Pitt and Goulburn Streets.
For a dine-dance place (costly because of a big band and top imported talent), the food, Chinese and Occidental, is excellent. Book, but you'll still have to queue. Worth it.

CHUCK WAGON, William Street.
Fun place, great atmosphere, but a bit rough. Excellent bistro fare. Great rough house wines. Cheap. Sydney distilled. Gentlemen must not remove thongs.

DOYLE'S PIER, on the Harbour at Rose Bay.
Possibly one of the world's great seafood meals. Huge portions. Above all, eat prawn cutlets. Take your own libations. Would rate higher, but enormous crowds make this a bit of a food factory. Worth the discomfort.

THE FRENCH RESTAURANT, Taylor Square.
Very French, from the brown onion soup to the strolling minstrels. Excellent food, pleasant ambience.

THE GOLDEN GRILL, Chevron Hotel.
A classic hotel grill room. They should all be run this way. Top "pop-in" rendezvous. Very wide menu, agreeable atmosphere, good service; very reasonable.

HUNTERS LODGE, Cross Street, Double Bay.
Dine-dance. See and meet the "beautiful young people". Casual, comfortable. Tasty food at moderate prices. The "in" joint, till fashions change.

THE INN OF THE GOLDEN OX, Regent Street.
The great beef will make you forgive the pretentious title. Steaks, roast beef, all the beef refinements. Costly.

Bored with the best of restaurant lunches? Take a picnic to the Hawkesbury River, just beyond Sydney's northern suburbs. Better still, live on a chartered cruiser like this, and enjoy Australia's most serene holiday.

👑👑👑 **JAPANESE NAGOYA SUKIYAKI HOUSE,** Victoria Street, King's Cross.
Fine ethnic dishes, served with charm, a smile, and a real desire to please. Reasonable.

👑👑👑👑 **LE TRIANON,** Challis Avenue, King's Cross.
A little more charm in the room, and a little less crowding, and this could be Sydney's greatest. Ultimate French cuisine, great oysters. Expensve.

👑👑👑 **MOTHER'S CELLAR,** Elizabeth Bay Road, King's Cross.
Not a single unfortunate item on the menu, so you'll find it very hard to keep room for the house specialty, superb pancakes. Try. Inexpensive.

👑👑👑 **PRIMO'S,** Elizabeth Bay Road, Elizabeth Bay.
Italian cuisine; very intimate and comfortable. Moderate prices.

👑👑👑 **PRUNIER,** Double Bay.
Elegant, costly, very good. Haute cuisine, with especially good seafoods.

👑👑👑 **SLAMAT MAKAN,** Victoria Street, Darlinghurst.
Indonesian ethnic dishes tempt the jaded appetite. The real thing, very well done. Moderate prices.

👑👑👑 **SUMMIT,** Australia Square Tower.
Revolving restaurant high in the sky. A shattering experience at twilight. Service poor, food good. Expensive.

For a gourmet treat, fish the cold clear waters of the Snowy Mountains at Lake Eucumbene. Toss a fresh, fat rainbow trout in flour, fry lightly in salted butter with some new-ground black pepper and a squeeze of lemon. An epicurean delight. Eat it with crusty handmade bread, and the white wine of your choice. The Snowys are a day's run from Sydney. Marvel at the majesty of the world's biggest hydro-electric and irrigation scheme, where rivers run in man-directed courses carrying the thundering waters of the Australian Alps; and delight in beauty like this.

WHERE TO LIVE IN SYDNEY

AUSTRALIA HOTEL, Castlereagh Street.
Traditional hotel, valiant efforts made to update accommodation. Central location at absolute heart of city. Moderate licensed restaurant, 24-hour room service. Expensive.

CHEVRON HOTEL, King's Cross, 1 mile from city.
Best-located hotel in Australia. Theatre-restaurant. Ask for high room on either side, for superlative views of city or Harbour. Rooftop suites, though very expensive, command thrilling views. Impressive 24-hour room service. Excellent grill room for lunches. Make memories by watching the city being lashed with rain at midnight, over a hamburger and champagne supper. Or enjoy fresh flounder fillets for breakfast with the whole harbour at your feet. Some rooms are shabby.

KOALA PARK REGIS MOTEL, Park Street.
New tower at heart of city, breathtaking views. Pool, 24-hour room service, licensed restaurant. Moderate tariff.

MACLEAY STREET TRAVELODGE MOTEL, King's Cross, 1 mile from city.
Ask for high room with harbour views. Pool, licensed restaurant; opposite Chevron Hotel.

RUSHCUTTER TRAVELODGE MOTEL, Rushcutter's Bay, $1\frac{1}{2}$ miles from city.
Ask for high room overlooking Rushcutter's Bay. Excellent pool, rooftop restaurant with fine harbour views. Expensive.

More great trout fishing in SE New South Wales' Murrumbidgee River. Quiet in autumn, in spring it carries melted snows from the Australian Alps 1,500 miles to the oceans of South Australia, irrigating as it goes.

♕♕♕♕   **TOWN HOUSE MOTEL,** Elizabeth Bay, near King's Cross.
Out-of-town, quiet, spacious; and beautifully designed. The business man's favourite. Many thoughtful extras. 24-hour room service, good licensed restaurant. Expensive.

♕♕♕♕♕   **WENTWORTH HOTEL,** Phillip Street.
At heart of city and theatreland. Unusual half-moon architecture. Thoughtful provision of all the "little extras". Excellent licensed restaurant and grill rooms. Lush, spacious lounges. Good music for dancing, great piano bar. Impeccable 24-hour room service.

♕♕♕♕   **WHITEHALL HOTEL MOTEL,** Rushcutter's Bay, 1½ miles from city.
Ask for high room on Harbour side. Excellent licensed restaurant. 24-hour room service. Very comfortable.

MELBOURNE, *population 2¼ million, capital of the State of Victoria, population three and one-third million.*
Between Melbourne and Sydney there exists what is said to be a 'good-natured rivalry.' Actually, it's a bit of parochial chauvinism, so fervid as to be pretty damned sick, of which both cities are equally guilty. In fine, the situation is that Melbourne people are petty jealous of the virtues of Sydney; dynamism, iconoclasm, tolerance, gaiety, extroversion . . . while Sydney-siders are petty jealous of those virtues that are special to Melbourne; stability, charm, peace, conservatism, introversion, introspection . . .

It's a sick thing because it's carried to the extremes of making the people of both cities lose sight of the fact that there is a nation of three million square miles out there . . . called Australia.

Sydney is run by smart young money, making silk Cardin-

". . . those virtues that are special to Melbourne . . ." ⟩
Including ample open spaces; room to live, breathe and play. City's skyline crowns vista over Albert Park lake, dotted with serene Saturday sailers.

suited decisions in far-out boardrooms; Melbourne is run by safe old money, making wool Saville Row-suited decisions from the scotch-in-hand, secure deeps of hide armchairs in discreet, powerful clubs.

Sydney is permissive, and topless go-go is unexceptional; Melbourne is pruriently prudish, and has a police-state fervour about 'immorality' . . . a bared navel is heralded as the Devil's shaft aimed at unsullied youth, nipples are ordered painted off magazine foldouts as though this expunging will make the vile things go away, and bannings are repeatedly ordered, to the gross embarrassment of most of what is, at heart, a liberal community. A plaster figleaf was mooted for a replica of Michelangelo's 'David' (possibly the most perfect work of art since man rose from the swamps) at the behest of a vocal few of the shopping-baggers of Melbourne; but happily David's superb explicitness was saved for Melbourne's contemporary scene by a director of the displaying emporium, a red-headed Irishman who struck a blow for freedom by declaiming 'No fig leaf; this would make us the laughing stock of the world.'

Melbourne is a delightful city, as big as West Berlin; and as calm and serene as its murky Yarra River. There's not much noise at night, for a simple and very sound reason; Melbourne people are content people, whose values are simply based. They are *good* values; love of home, love of garden, love of sun, love of football . . . and love of "telly."

Melbourne is the heart of Australia's finance and industry, and befittingly it has Australia's finest art collection, coasting somewhat on past acquisitional glories, and housed in a lavish new 'Arts Centre.' It also has endless handsome parks and gardens, and a delightful outdoor Music Bowl, where 100,000 can picnic on the green lawns and listen to 'Music for the People' programmes, free.

Melbourne hosted a successful Olympiad whose by-product was a great sporting complex, a few hundred yards from the city's heart. On the main arena, since enlarged, 125,000 people shout themselves into frenzy at the annual Australian Rules Football Final, a kind of aerial gladiatorial clash with a football . . . grand to watch.

". . . content people, whose values are simply based." Budding ballerinas share their moments of virginal grace with their teacher. The stage: Melbourne's Royal Botanic Gardens. Their spotlight: pearly golden sunshine. Their music: a thousand birds.

Most Melbourne arteries, as a gesture to that celebrated moribundity-inducing innate conservatism, carry trams; square-wheeled clattering charmless juggernauts, which pass along less than a safe car's-width from parked vehicles, and slow the moving flood of traffic to a ritual six miles per hour. On the occasions when their crews strike, Melbourne is a city transformed . . . ulcers cease to trouble and much business can be transacted.

The trams are ruinously expensive, and because of the unimaginatively-unstaggered business closing-times, at peak periods they take on all the aspects of mobile charnel houses.

Avoid them!

Most Melbourne suburban trains are cluttered with rubbish and defaced by vandals.

Melbourne is a good city for taxis, which are in the main clean and efficient; and your driver may well be a fifty-ish auntie, uniformed and courteous.

Melbourne hotel food is with few exceptions mediocre but the city's *good* restaurants are splendid and leave Sydney's best for dead. The Italian cuisine is especially good, perhaps Australia's best.

About Melbourne's climate . . . the city has only half Sydney's rainfall, but it has long days sitting under acutely depressing, insistent, leaking grey cloud; depressing to business, depressing to the human spirit . . . just plain depressing. Surprisingly, Sydney annually doesn't get much more sun than Melbourne (although Melbourne gets least of all the capitals); but the two climates seem to this writer to bear a significant relationship to the personalities of the citizens. Melbourne putters along dejectedly under grey skies; but even when Sydney greys, tumultuous things happen; lightning, thunder . . . slashing tropical rainstorms.

Shopping? Melbourne is Australia's fashion centre, so buy elegant fashions, particularly sensibly-svelte wool suits, skirts and jackets. The young designers' fashions are cheekily chic. The city arcades harbour hundreds of boutiques and specialty shops, giving great value now that they feel threatened by the trend to suburban shopping.

". . . long days sitting under acutely depressing, insistent, leaking grey cloud." Melbourne toilers pack city's Flinders Street station during winter evening peak. Open fires, good hot dinners, slippers and telly give their feet wings.

A certain Melbourne fashion store is Australia's most graciously elegant.

Melbourne's Flemington is regarded as the 'headquarters' of Australian horse-racing.

The spring racing carnival, in late October-early November, is Australia's greatest series of meetings, with crowds often hovering in the six figures. Melbourne people (particularly the supremely autocratic club that runs the course) are smug about Flemington, and consider it the world's finest racecourse; but Flemington's facilities, if transferred to a great many overseas courses, would be considered of pie-stall standard; and the spring carnival is marred by a singularly incongruous contest called 'Fashions in the Field', which started as an elegant conception but currently functions as a graceless outlet for fashion extremes, whose bared breasts and thighs distract from excellent racing. Unctuous garment industry public relations groups vie to steal each other's thunder by importing far-out beauties who jet into Melbourne from all the world, like a mid-October flight of exquisite locusts.

But the course is very, very spacious and immaculately groomed, the horses are good, the flowers magnificent; and on Derby Day, when the ladies other than the fashion contestants are their elegant best, and the garment industry procurers and gentlemen affect morning suits and grey toppers, Flemington represents Melbourne at her reasonable, gentle, genteel best. Become a guest at a chicken and champagne picnic 'Under the Elms', or a pie and beer picnic 'on the Hill', on Derby Day . . . great fun.

Sandown is a newer, more pleasantly designed course.

Forget being naughty in Melbourne. There is much naughtiness, but it's very sleazy. Heavy-handed self-righteousness turns naughtiness into vice, and Melbourne vice is of a singularly unpleasant kind.

Melbourne's social establishment is unselectively based on two criteria, worthiness and the possession of money, however gained.

"*. . . Flemington represents Melbourne at her rea-*
sonable, gentle, genteel best." **Proud jockey brings a**
Derby winner in along a lane of roses. Course is
immaculately groomed for Spring Carnival of four
meetings in eight days.

WHERE TO EAT IN MELBOURNE

ANTONIO'S, Toorak Road, South Yarra.
Very good, very expensive. But charmless room keeps it short of ultimate.

BEEFEATER, Carlisle Street, Balaclava.
Great roast beef, great steaks, great cheeses. But service indifferent.

EDOUARD, Toorak Road, South Yarra.
Good food with piquant sauces; perhaps a little feminine. Excellent menu, moderate prices.

FANNY'S, Lonsdale Street.
Often overcrowded, but real gourmet fare at prices bordering on expensive. Great for rich sauces; house wines indifferent.

FLORENTINO, Bourke Street.
As dependable as the day is long. Superior Italian cuisine, very friendly ambience. And that rarity . . . a genuine desire to serve. 2 rooms, 2 menus, 2 prices.

FLORENTINO BISTRO, Bourke Street.
Barbecue steaks at moderate prices. Good carafe house wines (try the burgundy). Perhaps Australia's tastiest barbecued grills. Recommended.

GINA'S BISTRO, Lygon Street, Carlton.
Genuine Italian home cooking. Pleasant room, good cellar, moderate prices.

GOLDEN PHOENIX, Exhibition Street.
Overlit, but perhaps Australia's best Chinese restaurant. Use fingers on Crisp Skin Chicken, your meal finishes with fragrant hot towel.

Buy take-away food at nearby Toorak Road, South Yarra, especially from La Krokette or L'Escargot; and eat it in the Royal Botanic Gardens or here, on the Yarra bank. A Sunday delight, and fine fare.

HUNTERS LODGE, Dorset Road, Croydon.
Away out of town, but if your choice is for robust fare, downed with much stein-thumping to a Teutonic singalong, this is for you. Book.

LAMPLIGHTER, Bourke Street.
Handy basement room, good but not great. Moderate prices, cosy.

LATIN, Lonsdale Street.
Traditional Italian menu. Consistently very good. Moderate prices.

LAZAR, Little Bourke Street.
Elaborate (Hollywood-Medieval) decor, rickety slate tables, pretentious menus. Inconsistent. Good music. An experience.

LE CHATEAU, Queens Road.
Profligate extravagance of decor has to be paid for . . . by the diners. Perhaps Australia's most expensive French food, but very good. Dinner dance, vast wine list. An expense-account joint.

L'ESCARGOT, Toorak Road, South Yarra.
Traditional French. Real home cooking. Casseroles are especially good. Cheap, takeaway service

LITTLE REATA, Little Collins Street.
Rough-hewn decor.   Food is better than its cousin's, Lazar. Great Smorgasbord luncheon.

MAXIM'S, Toorak Road, South Yarra.
Great the day it opened its doors, great ever since. Australia's best. French, of course. Expensive.

MAXIM'S, Bourke Street.
Vying to shake its sister restaurant's lead, but ambience of room lets it down a little. Food superb. Expensive.

Chef at Southern Cross hotel proffers laden platter of grills, for cooking to your choice. Bustling hotel maintains high standard. Try its coffee shop, The Coolabah, especially for Melbourne's best and cheapest Sunday lunch.

MAYFAIR ROOM (Southern Cross Hotel), Exhibition Street.
A charming, big room, especially pleasant for lunch. Band too noisy at dine-dance, detracts from really fine food.

ORIENTAL GOURMET, Little Bourke Street.
Melbourne's other great Chinese restaurant. Ask for chef's specials. Personal, friendly service. Costly.

OXFORD, Swanston Street.
Had its ups and downs, but now serving fine food, very fresh. Delightful room, quiet and comfortable.

PELLEGRINI'S, Bourke Street.
Two rooms. Front is snack bar, back is hot and cold buffets. An Italian food factory, but tasty, hot, and in incredible variety, different hourly. Choose yourself. Cheap.

PORTERHOUSE, Toorak Road, South Yarra.
Just plain consistent, tasty, moderately priced, satisfying meals. Unexceptional room. Very good value.

PICKWICK, Toorak Road, South Yarra.
Dine-dance in a nice, cosy ambience. Olde-worlde, currently the darling of the mini-jet setters. Reasonable prices.

SOCIETY, Bourke Street.
Yet another of the traditional Italian places that Melbourne has in such abundance. Long-established, very consistent; reasonable prices.

SUKIYAKI, Alfred Place.
Probably Australia's leading Japanese restaurant. Gracious, hospitable, unusual. Expensive, because some of their ingredients travel thousands of miles.

Traditional love of Melbourne people for their homes is shared by young hostesses like fashion designer Prue Acton. She shuns restaurants for entertaining; prefers good food, good talk, candle-lit intimacy of her own dining-room.

TWO FACES, Toorak Road, South Yarra.
Swiss-French, for when you have that jaded feeling for "something different". Good service, pleasant room.

TOLARNO FRENCH BISTRO, Fitzroy Street, St. Kilda.
Noisy and overpriced, but excellent food. Good cellar, but house wines poor. If rubbing shoulders with artists is your thing . . . then this is for you. Gallery annexed. Onion soup, provincial casseroles are great.

VLADO'S CHARCOAL GRILL, Bridge Road, Richmond.
Excellent salads served with probably the biggest steaks south of the Equator, and great barbecued continental pork sausages. Bring potables. Expensive.

WALNUT TREE, William Street.
Unusual room with good French and Italian food. Inconsistent, but worth a try. When it's good, it's great.

WHERE TO STAY IN MELBOURNE

AUSTRALIA HOTEL, Collins Street.
Traditional hotel, oldish, right at city heart. Licensed restaurant, 24-hour room service, grill room, bistro, snack rooms. Moderate to expensive.

COMMODORE DOWNTOWNER, Lygon Street, Carlton.
Unattractive suburban surroundings, so this Commodore is turned inside-out (blind brick exterior, centre court). Attractive, comfortable suites. Unlicensed, reasonable.

Within three blocks north of Melbourne's Town Hall (peeping from behind city Christmas tree at right) you will find, especially in Bourke Street, literally scores of good restaurants. But many in Collins Street are capable of pleasing; try them too.

COMMODORE MOTEL, Queens Road.
A little noisy, on apex of road junction. Pleasant suites overlook park if you ask for them. Good licensed restaurant. Moderate tariffs.

JOHN BATMAN TRAVELLODGE MOTEL, Queens Road.
Pleasant location near Albert Park Lake. Excellent licensed restaurant, moderate tariffs.

PALM LAKE MOTOR INN, Queens Road.
Moderate to excellent suites. Ask for high room on lake side. Pool, fair restaurant. Golf course. Conventions sometimes noisy.

PARKROYAL MOTOR INN, Royal Parade, Parkville.
Quiet, comfortable parkside location. Pool, excellent licensed restaurant with pleasant ambience. Moderate to expensive. New wing is very quiet.

PRESIDENT MOTOR INN, Queens Road.
New, roomy, comfortable. Suites especially fine. 24-hour room service, good licensed restaurant. Moderate tariffs. Ask for high room overlooking lake.

QUEENSLODGE MOTOR INN, Queens Road.
Very new; ask for high room with lake view. Suites are superb. 24-hour room service, excellent licensed restaurant. Moderate to expensive.

SHERATON MOTOR HOTEL, Spring Street.
Small rooms with gracious views of Fitzroy Gardens. Good licensed restaurant. Costly to very expensive.

Take a basket of goodies to Sherbrooke Forest, in the Dandenongs, an hour east of Melbourne. Have the picnic of your life in a fern gully. If it's strawberry time, augment your lunch with a couple of fresh punnets from the hills farms. Sprinkle with castor sugar and a little brandy, and dip in fresh hills cream. Delicious.

👑👑👑👑 **SOUTHERN CROSS HOTEL**, Exhibition Street.

This hotel would rate with the highest were its outlook not onto a million dreary rooftops (but charming by night). International hotel with American-style suites, service and management. Centre-city. 24-hour room service. Good restaurants, grill rooms, snack rooms; but very crowded at peak periods. Expensive.

👑👑👑 **WINDSOR HOTEL,** Spring Street.

Olde-worlde, gracious, elegant, roomy and comfortable. Slightly down-at-heel in an appealing way. 24-hour room service, licensed restaurant. Parliament House is opposite.

CANBERRA, *population 101,000, National Capital of Australia.*

Canberra is tucked away in a pocket in the Australian Alps, where it was put as an uneasy geographical compromise gesture to the jealousies of Melbourne and Sydney. It should have been put on the coast, to the east.

Canberra is sunny, beautifully planned and executed, clean to the point of being antiseptic, and bitterly cold on many mornings. Federal Parliament sits here, and may be viewed in action, that the viewer may make his own decisions about the quality of Australian oratory and debating. Most of Canberra's population works in the Commonwealth Public Service, or in foreign embassies or legations (many of them characterised by architectural flamboyance, the better to reflect the cultures or aspirations of their incumbents).

The War Memorial is a museum of epic proportions, chronicling Australia's part in actions the world over, and storing the banners, hardware and artifacts used in those hostilities.

"Canberra is sunny, beautifully planned and executed, clean to the point of being antiseptic...." City abounds in parks and (especially considerate) squares furnished with comfortable seats; warm wind-shielded sun-traps.

Most of the educational and scientific authorities headquartered in Canberra welcome visitors, and tourism is the city's most valuable source of outside income. Hotels are fair, motor-hotels excellent, most restaurants poor. Theatre is meagre, but excellent. Art is all-but non-existent, but projected on a grand scale. Be taken into somebody's home, or travel in company . . . to do otherwise is to remain friendless. Canberra is very beautiful, and full of interest; but as yet without warmth. Amble through the Australian National University, Australia's most serenely beautiful campus; and picnic daily (on excellent delicatessen things) atop Black Mountain, or on the shores of Lake Burley Griffin (named after the American who designed basic Canberra), where classic public buildings shimmer sunnily in blue aspic reflections. Beautiful, and quietly pride-stirring.

The writer gives the back of his hand to those who dub Canberra 'a poor man's Brasilia', and owns to frank old-fashioned patriotic pride when he spends time there.

Canberra's social establishment is predicated on what position a person occupies in what peck order.

WHERE TO EAT IN CANBERRA

BACCHUS TAVERN, Hobart Place.
Excellent French food in pleasant downstairs room. Reasonable prices.

CHESTER FORD (Travelodge Motel), Northbourne Avenue.
Good food served piping hot by pretty "serving wenches". Cosy panelled room, reasonable prices, good wines.

NOAH'S (Town House Motel), Rudd Street.
Superlative cuisine, delightful room, impeccable service.

"Australian National University, Australia's most serenely beautiful campus. . . ." Wholesome, happy teenagers trundle off to lectures on their scooter. Building is School of General Studies library, one of university's many library divisions.

WHERE TO STAY IN CANBERRA

CANBERRA-REX   HOTEL,   Northbourne Avenue.
City's premier hotel. Pool, excellent licensed restaurant and lounges. 24-hour room service. Moderate to expensive tariffs. New wing is quietest.

CANBERRA   CITY   TRAVELODGE MOTEL, Northbourne Avenue.
Pool, private balconies, excellent fresh-air conditioning. Fine restaurant on ground floor. Reasonable tariff. High rooms are sunnier and quieter.

PARKROYAL MOTOR INN, Northbourne Avenue.
In tradition of excellent Parkroyal chain. Quiet, comfortable, excellent value, rather expensive. Stroll to city's heart.

TOWN HOUSE MOTOR INN, Rudd Street.
Impressive, unusual architecture. Very comfortable and central. 24-hour room service, and Noah's restaurant forms part. Moderate tariff.

BRISBANE, *population 800,000, capital of the State of Queensland, population 1,800,000.*
    An amiable city, Brisbane, with a year-through summer temperature, populated by a happy-go-lucky, all-but-indolent, engaging lot. The houses, generally innocent of paint, stilt-borne like Javanese canal-shanties, look mostly as though they should burn down; yet many of them have a kind of flower-dappled charm that recalls the U.S. deep south, with overtones of

At Brisbane's back door, a twenty-mile long beach-fringed fantasy; the Gold Coast. Australia's biggest holiday resort basks in a 77-degree daily average temperature. Pale skins turn to gold in 290 days of sunshine each year.

Tennessee Williams. Of course there are exceptions; this writer loves the bustle of the Brisbane River as seen from Hamilton Heights, and as near as darn-it bought a 2½-acre block on that same river at Figtree Pocket a couple of years ago.

Queensland's dear old State Government endlessly pours out promotional material on Queensland's potential, and in fact the State is dynamic and very much on the move. A pity the State capital doesn't reflect this dynamism; it is torpid and quite relentlessly ugly. The writer thinks the climate is to blame; it's mostly magnificent, but often enervatingly humid, bereft of the ritual winds that relieve most hot Australian cities on clammy afternoons . . . a climate to quieten the physical ardour of the most zealous.

The hotels are frightful, but the motor-hotels good. Hotel food is frankly beyond belief, but restaurants are excellent. Particularly, eat Queensland beef, probably Australia's best. Cinemas are good, live theatre only fair, night life poor, art poor. Brisbane people tend to have swimming pools, and spend evenings in or near them . . . which *is* a pretty nice idea when you think of it. They slip away to the Gold Coast to blow off steam.

Shopping in Brisbane is mediocre.

Queensland is chock-full of wonderful things and places, but Brisbane (though it would be a fine place to call 'home') is a good city to pass through as fleetingly as one can contrive, if proceeding either north or south.

For a laugh, don't miss the airport, a cross between a white-painted army camp and Cuban sugar warehouses. There are always a couple of 'Sunbirds', superannuated DC3's with engines missing and heads lowered between their knees, shimmering by the taxi-ways, so one knows instantly what a Bolivian airport looked like in 1934.

Perhaps in ten years, when some of that potential is realised, Brisbane will more fittingly represent the magnificent State of Queensland.

Brisbane's social establishment is predicated on where one lives, and the size of one's swimming pool.

Little pockets of enchantment in the form of protected rain-forests dot the mountains behind the Brisbane-Gold Coast complex. This is Natural Arch, an hour's drive inland from Surfers Paradise. Take a chicken and a bottle of hock; picnic.

WHERE TO EAT IN BRISBANE

ANGUS STEAKHOUSE (National Hotel), Queen Street.
Great steaks, from the best of Queensland's fine beef.

CAMELIA, Queen Street.
Continental-Australian; exceptional cellar.

CHEZ TESSA, Wickham Terrace.
Genuine Italian fare, and lashings of it. Comfortable, charming. Moderate prices.

LEO'S, Edward Street.
Fine food in an elegant roof-garden atop the city. Expensive, very good.

LITTLE TOKYO, Charlotte Street.
Excellent ethnic dishes, served with exquisite grace by pretty Japanese hostesses.

MAMMA LUIGI'S, St. Paul's Terrace.
The BIG Italian dinner for lusty appetites. Unappealing surroundings, but the food's the thing.

ROOM AT THE TOP, Tower Mill Motel, Wickham Terrace.
Go for the 360 degree view, stay to enjoy really fine food, elegantly served. Twilight an experience.

Make whole meals of Queensland's fruit, Australia's finest, and very cheap. Fruit thought exotic in most of the world abounds here; rough-leaf pineapples, mangoes, paw-paws, bananas, banana passion-fruit and custard apples. For a few cents enjoy a gourmet delight, avocado with seafoods. Another special: Monstera Deliciosa, ripe and sun-warmed.

WHERE TO LIVE IN BRISBANE

ALBERT PARK MOTEL, Gregory and Wickham Terraces.
Quiet, out-of-town, gentle neighbourhood. 24-hour room service, unlicensed restaurant, pool, private balcony. Expensive.

CORONATION MOTEL, Riverside Drive.
Spacious, very modern; ask for high room overlooking Brisbane River. Unlicensed restaurant, 24-hour room service, moderate rates.

LENNONS HOTEL, George Street.
Brisbane's big one, seen better days. Fair food, noisy, very central. Licensed restaurant, 24-hour room service, expensive.

REGAL MOTEL, Alice Street.
Very central, yet overlooking the superb tropical Botanic Gardens. Unlicensed restaurant, pool, moderate tariff.

SOUTH PACIFIC MOTEL, Bowen Terrace.
Out-of-town, on park and river; homely. No restaurant, cooking facilities in suite. Reasonable rates.

TOWER MILL MOTEL, Wickham Terrace.
Fascinating round tower dominating city. Comfortable suites, private balconies, excellent rooftop restaurant. Expensive.

TRAVELODGE MOTEL, Kangaroo Point.
Out-of-town, very quiet. Ask for a high suite over the river, and you'll have Brisbane's most delightful accommodation. Pool, private balcony. Fine rooftop restaurant. Charming ferry to the city for a few cents.

Grab a steak or take a picnic to Surfers Paradise Gardens, tucked in on the Nerang River 15 minutes from the Gold Coast's Broadbeach. Ski yourself, or watch world champions in action during the daily ski show. Spectacular! Learn to ski at Surfside 6.

ABOUT 50 MILES south of Brisbane, along a fine highway, lies Australia's most extraordinary resort phenomenon, the Gold Coast, and its "capital", Surfers Paradise.

Surfers, building at an annual rate of $30 million, is, after Canberra, the fastest growing city in Australia. There are twenty miles of beaches in the Gold Coast complex; twenty miles of shimmering, silky white sand, lapped by 72 degree surf, and basking in a 77-degree average temperature. The sun blazes down on these beaches for 290 days of every 365.

Aesthetically, Surfers is "bloody murder," but one should remember that it is essentially a permissive, happy, fun place; roaring with life and colour. A kind of Queensland Miami.

Millions of Australians holiday on the Coast, and there is much to divert one from one's big-capital cipherism.

Brisbaneites can run down in an hour or so, often just for an interesting evening meal, or an afternoon in the quite incredible Surfers Paradise Hotel beer garden, or a great night out.

Typists come to Surfers for ten-day holidays, and manage by ingenuity and hard work to spin their stays out to a worldly-wise six months, before going home to unknowing boy-friends, secure in banks.

The inns and wells of the Gold Coast put their Brisbane cousins to shame, so they bear description. In other words, do what almost everybody does. See Brisbane, then go to Surfers Paradise.

WHERE TO EAT AT SURFERS PARADISE

BISTRO CELLAR, Cavill Avenue.
Gold Coast's best classic bistro food. Open char-grill, choose your steak. Inexpensive.

CAPTAIN'S TABLE, Cavill Avenue.
A seafood heaven. Gives the lie to the suggestion that Queensland's seafoods are generally poor. Reasonable.

"Meter Maids", the goldenest girls in all the world, protect errant drivers from parking tickets at expired meters along Surfers Paradise kerbs. Benevolent local merchants supply coins, pay infinitely decorative maids.

♕♕♕ **COPENHAGEN,** Mermaid Beach.
Selected Scandinavian and European dishes. Very good fare at moderate prices.

♕♕♕ **EL RANCHO BAR-B-Q,** Cavill Avenue.
Could possibly be Australia's best and cheapest barbecue. Eat great steaks or chicken in the best possible decor . . . under tropical trees.

♕♕♕ **GOLDEN PEACOCK ROOM,** Chevron Hotel.
Opulent hotel room, dine-dance. Good music, moderate food. Expensive.

♕♕♕ **GREEN DRAGON,** Cavill Avenue.
Great Chinese food, ask for chef's specials. Inexpensive.

♕♕♕♕ **HIBISCUS ROOM** (Margot Kelly's), Hanlan Street.
International cuisine, elegant room and service. But strolling players are obtrusive. Dance. Expensive.

♕♕♕♕ **HIGH BONNET,** Pacific Highway.
Excellent home-style cooking. Baron of beef an event. Moderate prices.

♕♕♕♕ **JOLLY FROG,** Pacific Highway.
Best French cuisine on the Coast. Fun place, moderate.

♕♕♕♕ **KEITH'S,** Cavill Avenue.
Great steaks from charcoal grill; pleasant, cool room. Recommended. Pricey.

♕♕♕ **L'APERITIF,** Laycock Street.
Try delicate steaks cooked at your table. Dance. Good music, moderate prices.

♕♕♕ **PARADISE ROOM,** Surfers Paradise Hotel.
Cool, elegant, spacious and very good. Expensive hotel room. Book. Dance to just-right music.

Picnic on the beach at Surfers Paradise, but achieve your best-ever tan without burn, protected by (and this is true) a generous sprayed coat of mutton-bird oil! For a few cents, a golden glow.

WHERE TO STAY AT SURFERS PARADISE

BROADBEACH HOTEL, Oceanfront, Broadbeach.

Set in seven acres of glorious tropical gardens 2 miles from Surfers Paradise. Huge pool, private balconies. Ask for high room on east side, and have your dinner served on the balcony for a twilight treat. 24-hour room service, licensed restaurant. Costly.

BUCKINGHAM MOTEL, Laycock Street.

Breakfast served, and luncheon-making facilities in excellent suites, evening meal service from adjacent restaurant. Heated pool. Moderate tariff, quiet location off highway, near surf beach.

CHEVRON PARADISE HOTEL, Ferny Avenue.

Two huge pools, set in tropical gardens. Request pool-side room, others disappointing. 24-hour room service, excellent restaurants, snack facilities. Music everywhere.

FLAMINGO MOTEL, Hanlan Street.

Comfortable suites, pool. No restaurant, but fine food brought in from Margot Kelly's, next door. Costly.

PINK POODLE MOTEL, Gold Coast Highway.

Delightful architecture. Would have rated higher, but highway location can be pretty noisy. Unlicensed restaurant, pool. Tariffs . . . cheap to moderate.

SANDS MOTOR INN, Esplanade.

Pool, unlicensed restaurant, right on the beach. High rooms have unequalled view of Gold Coast beaches. Moderate to costly. Penthouse suites a delight.

A whirlpool of feathered colour, as thousands of lorikeets come to dinner at Currumbin sanctuary at south end of Gold Coast. Picnic on the beach, and in mid-afternoon feed the birds with your own personal plate of bread and honey.

ADELAIDE, *population 790,000, capital of the State of* *South Australia, population 1,125,000.*
Adelaide's charm average is considerably elevated by avenues of graceful colonial sandstone houses, set in leafy gardens which always manage to look pleasant despite ferocious water restrictions. The city sits on a flat littoral, backed by the Mount Lofty Ranges, which are an autumnal delight; and there are substantial sanctuary areas in which kangaroos, emus and other fauna go free, in hundreds—and honestly do eat from the hands of picnicking visitors; all this only three or four miles from the city's heart.

Australia's' biggest cultural festivals happen in Adelaide, and, although aberrations occur, by and large they are *true* cultural festivals of great interest and very, very high standard.

Hotels are moderate, motor-hotels excellent, restaurants excellent. Drink wine, copiously; it is Australia's best, from the nearby Barossa Valley . . . and a house carafe of wine is better than export quality, particularly in the colorful cellar bistros.

Adelaide's art gallery is excellent, with an encouraging cosy *ambience* missing from more elaborate galleries.

Eat fish and crustacea, flown in fresh daily from nearby Port Lincoln.

Shopping is good, and boutiques abound in the arcades, one of which, an extraordinary edifice, reminds one of a Moscow GUM store. North Adelaide, a few cents away by bus, is the home of astonishingly good antique shops, galleries, restaurants and rare-wine stores.

Adelaide is a graceful, gentle city, with a sparkling, sunny climate; and boating on the Torrens River, right at the heart of the city, brings a delicate touch of tranquillity.

The beaches are moderate, and the night-life indifferent.

Driving is easy and unruffled, as are taxis.

A prosperous, comfortable city, with inborn breeding and dignity.

Adelaide's social establishment is predicated on *whether one went to* that *school, or married one of its* *issue.*

> **From Adelaide, join a tour or drive north for 90** **minutes to the Barossa Valley. Picnic at vineyards;** **inspect wineries, try and buy Australia's finest wines.** **The Barossa will give you a memorable day.**

WHERE TO EAT IN ADELAIDE

👑👑👑 **ARKABA RED WINE GRILL,** Glen Osmond Road, Fullarton.
Lush big room, unobtrusive music. Excellent beef and seafoods; fine wines from the renowned Barossa Valley. Moderate prices. Out of town.

👑👑👑 **ARKABA STEAK CELLAR,** Gilbert Place.
Cosy cellar decor, rough-hewn furniture. Excellent sizzling barbecue, great red wines. For lunch and dinner. Moderate prices.

👑👑👑👑 **DECCA'S PLACE,** Melbourne Street, North Adelaide.
Unusually pleasant room on Adelaide's north side. Especially eat seafoods and drink recommended white wines, Barossa Valley's best.

👑👑👑👑 **ERNEST'S,** on the Torrens River.
Enchanting room suspended over the river at Adelaide's heart. True international standard; expensive.

👑👑👑 **SWAIN'S SEAFOOD RESTAURANT,** Glen Osmond Road, Frewville.
Adelaide's prime seafood comes from the teeming icy waters of the Southern Ocean. Superlatively treated here, at moderate prices.

To make memories, dine at Ernest's. If the night is balmy, sip your Barossa Valley wine on the terrace over the Torrens River. True Adelaide charm, bejewelled with the city's lights, just across the water. Ask the sommelier for his wine preference; it will be very good indeed.

WHERE TO STAY IN ADELAIDE

AUSTRALIA HOTEL, Brougham Place, North Adelaide, 1 mile from city.
Particularly ask for high room overlooking city; back rooms are claustrophobic cells. Superb 24-hour room service, excellent licensed restaurant with fine views. Expensive.

GROSVENOR HOTEL, North Terrace.
Very central, licensed restaurant, cheap.

PARKROYAL MOTOR INN, North Terrace.
Pool, sauna, good licensed restaurant. Ask for room overlooking park. Moderate tariff.

SOUTH AUSTRALIAN HOTEL, North Terrace.
Traditional, olde-worlde. Rooms are poor, suites good. Licensed restaurant, 24-hour room service. Expensive.

TRAVELODGE MOTEL, South Terrace.
Standard first-class motel. Pool, good licensed restaurant. Moderate tariff.

PERTH, *population 600,000, capital of the State of Western Australia, population pushing 1 million.*

As behooves the capital city of a State that has found itself in possession of a goodly-sized chunk of Australia's enormous new finds of mineral riches, Perth is where the development action is.

First striking things about Perth are its international air terminal and its international shipping terminal; both of them international in that they genuinely seem to welcome visitors and stand in striking contrast to the loathsome aggregations of sheds that pass for entrance facilities at most of Australia's gateways. Perth's airport is spacious, imaginative, parklike. Abundantly endowed with civilized touches, it even sports a gaggle of fat black swans (the State emblem) in a pond sited smack in the middle of the passenger complex.

"_. . . Perth is where the development action is._"
Landfall for migrants, beacon for astronauts, prosperous capital of Western Australia, Perth fulfils many roles. But it cherishes its reputation as Australia's "City of Lights", earned when pioneer astronaut John Glenn, in orbit through blackness, thirteen minutes and twenty-four seconds out of Zanzibar, gladdened the hearts of the people of Perth whose lights had been left burning overnight by saying "Just to my right I can see a big pattern of city lights, apparently right on the coast. The lights show up very well; thank everybody for turning them on, will you?"

The shipping terminal is spacious, airy, clean and, once again, abundantly endowed with civilized touches: it even sports a boothful of hostesses, coolly attractive multi-lingual beauties in cute red sailor suits who will answer your most irritatingly repetitious questions with interest, courtesy, and unexasperated charm.

Perth believes that the Lord helps those that help themselves. The city already has public parking space for thousands of cars above immediate requirements. Its people years ago put themselves completely in the hands of aesthetically skilled town-planners, and they are reaping the fluid, appealing, calm benefits. Perth, after Canberra, is the only capital that appears to be growing as the consequence of grand design.

Perth's university, at unfortunately-named Crawley, is splendid in conception and architecture, on a site carved in bushland, with millions of bright flowers.

The writer always recalls Perth as a city in which a million lush roses buoyantly bloom . . . you've never really seen roses triumphant till you've seen Perth's.

The city's climate is the most supremely genial of all the capitals, with an incredible average sunshine rate of 7.8 hours for every day of every year. In summer, when it can become very hot, yet still dry, there comes a wind, in mid-afternoon, called the 'Fremantle Doctor', from Perth's port on the Indian Ocean ten miles away, and this wind cools and soothes the city back to normalcy.

There are hundreds of outdoor eating establishments around Perth, where good, tasty food (particularly seafood) is sold for cents, in warmth, under the stars.

Hotels are mostly poor, motor-hotels good, restaurants good but not yet outstanding. Cinemas are good, live theatre poor, art poor.

Sailing on the Swan River (in places miles wide as it meanders to Fremantle) is a delight; as is a riverbank cook-out of fresh prawns, straight from the river.

Perth has its own wine, grown for U.K. export, but the writer suggests that you let the export trade prosper.

"Perth's university. . . . splendid in conception and architecture . . ." Students enjoy picnic lunch-break on lush, flower-embroidered lawns. Like most Perth things, university has room to breathe, grow; and soak in the abundant sun.

Perth people feel rather keenly the fact that they are a couple of deserts and a couple of thousand miles away from 'The East', a cliché they equate with the moon. They should actually hold still . . . their isolation has made them Australia's most charmingly unaffected people.

Perth's social establishment is predicated on how often one can afford to 'go East'.

WHERE TO EAT IN PERTH

EMBERS ROOM (Travelodge Motel), Terrace Drive.
Superb views over the Swan River augment an excellent menu. Try local wines with your steaks or seafoods (but only if recommended).

LUIS', Sherwood Court.
International cuisine of highest standard. Consistently good, superb service, very expensive.

THE TAVERN, Victoria Avenue, Claremont.
Out-of-town olde-worlde pub-style room. Very cosy, excellent beef. Moderate prices.

WILDFLOWER ROOM (Freeway Motel), Mill Point Road, South Perth.
Out-of-town, pleasant room in charming riverside location. Paintings of native W.A. wildflowers adorn walls of this serenely quiet room. Good food, moderate prices.

Picnic in Perth's delightful King's Park, or at a near-city roadside park. Your companions will be sunshine, birds and wildflowers. This is the aptly-named Kangaroo Paw, national flower of the State of Western Australia. Thousands of acres of Kangaroo Paws line roads in peak wildflower time; but there are a few about for most months of the year. Seeds are readily available at florists, souvenir shops, airport.

WHERE TO STAY IN PERTH

KOALA FREEWAY MOTEL, Mill Point Road, 1 mile from city.
Fine views of Swan River. Secluded and quiet. 24-hour room service, pool, licensed restaurant. Unusual and extremely pleasant architecture. Cheap; great value.

PALACE HOTEL, St. George's Terrace.
Right at city's heart. 24-hour room service, licensed restaurant, expensive.

PARMELIA HOTEL, Mill Street.
At city's heart. Brand new hotel, striving for world-standard ultimate in service and comfort. Expensive, but give yourself a treat. Reports not complete.

RIVERSIDE LODGE HOTEL, Mounts Bay Road.
Deceptive name. This is a top-notch motel tucked away at city's feet. Unusually sound design, very comfortable. Pool, 24-hour room service, good licensed restaurant. Costly.

TRAVELODGE MOTEL, Terrace Road.
Insist on high room overlooking Swan River. Low rooms are gloomy, noisy. Pool, good licensed restaurant with exceptional views. Cheap. Private balconies a delight.

Drive Western Australia's back roads, but be prepared for enormous distances. Do all the sensible things recommended by motoring organisations, but above all take abundant potables and a "tucker-box"; there could well be three, four or five hundred miles between you and replenishment! The roads are moderate, but enchantingly wattle-lined like this for many months of the year; and ambling through oceans of wildflowers for many others. Take two spare wheels; and never, never drive fast after twilight without a kangaroo-guard, or you'll likely find yourself with a faceful of 150-pound, 7-foot red kangaroo.

HOBART, *population 145,000, capital of the State of Tasmania, population 390,000.*

This enchanting little jewel of a city nestles under the protective lee of Mount Wellington, often snow-capped.

Hobart is Australia's southernmost, therefore chilliest, capital; but it is quite delightful enough to make one overlook its nippy air, which at times comes straight from the Antarctic with no barrier to its progress. The clean sweep of the Tasman Bridge links the two halves of Hobart flanking the Derwent Estuary, and Constitution Dock, right at the city's heart, is as picturesque and colorful as a Cape Cod movie set, or England's Penzance. Welled boats sell wriggling fresh fish to the city's burghers for transmission to abundant tables, for Hobart is prosperous.

The art gallery is a joy, with a good collection very appealingly hung; and it is married to an enchanting historical museum where old day books of the penal colony that was Tasmania and the cradle of Australia's history are open for examination. It comes as a shock to see the relics of 'the good old days', when silk-clad magisterial pillars of British probity ordered lashings, then transportation of boys and girls to Tasmania for life, for the most petty of offences, about equivalent to those which earn today's parking tickets.

For children of all ages there is a wonderful, wonderful ship room, with a ship's deck; and full of whaler's spears, flensing knives, carved whale-teeth, bravado-etchings of terrible ocean clashes, and leg-irons for recalcitrant impressed sailors . . . and a huge picture window overlooking Constitution Dock, with a binnacle and a windjammer's wheel taller than Captain Ahab; so that one can actually conn the entire city of Hobart out on to the Derwent, like a four-master heeling to the Roaring Forties!

Hobart has a fine folk museum, and treasure-filled antique shops.

Hotels are good, motor-hotels excellent. Bistro food is excellent. Whatever you do, eat seafoods . . . you are in the greatest seafood city in Australia, and the crayfish and scallops are unexcelled.

Hobart's social establishment is predicated on how one's forebears got to Hobart.

"*. . . an enchanting little jewel of a city. . . .*" **Pearl necklace of Tasman Bridge links Hobart's city proper with eastern suburbs, airport, and hundred-mile chain of holiday resorts and sleepy fishing villages; all unforgettably beautiful. Travel this east-coast road and live comfortably in excellent motels. Wash down the finest of Southern Ocean seafoods with crisp delight, new Mercury cider; memorable.**

WHERE TO EAT IN HOBART

BISTRO, Collins Street.
Fun cellar room with cosy decor, occasional strolling poets and players. Excellent choose-your-own-steak barbecue grill. Reasonable prices.

DIRTY DICK'S, Francis Street, Battery Point. Steak house in one of Australia's oldest suburbs. Historic ambience augments fine food. Reasonable prices.

DUTCH INN, Cromwell Street, Battery Point. Pleasant room steeped in historic Australiana. Fine food. Especially eat seafoods, fresh from the abundant nearby ocean.

WREST POINT, Sandy Bay.
Dine-dance, while picture windows bring Derwent Estuary to your table. Ring first; frequent dress-up nights can be dreary, prejudice good food and service.

WHERE TO STAY IN HOBART

TRAVELODGE MOTEL, Fountain Round-about.
High-standard motel. Most suites have park, estuary views. Ask for them. Unlicensed rooftop restaurant with superb aspect.

WREST POINT RIVIERA HOTEL, Sandy Bay Road, $1\frac{1}{2}$ miles from city.
Giant, slumbering hotel, soon to be galvanised as site of Australia's first legal casino. Ask for waterfront room. Excellent restaurant with estuary views.

". . . *Constitution Dock, right at the city's heart, is as picturesque and colourful as a Cape Cod movie set, or England's Penzance.*" The Battery Point restaurants (p. 78) sit high on the hill overlooking this delightful dock. Especially eat scallops, fresh from these boats which have trawled the icy clear waters of the D'Entrecasteaux Passage. Have them by the roadside, fresh from a twist of newspaper, crisply battered and deep-fried, and wash down with a bottle of dry cider. Or have them Provencal (in ramekins with garlic, butter, lemon juice and a little tomato puree with parsley) washed down with a recommended wine. Unforgettable. Fishing boats also bring fish and crayfish, fresh daily.

These are Australia's capital cities, seven and a quarter million souls deployed in elation, despair, unction, zeal, passion, passivity, rapture, hate, inertia, ambition, jealousy, conformity, lubricity, frigidity, activity; torpor and apathy, empathy and sympathy, death and birth . . . values common to cities the world over.

Yet in the capitals, like the rest of Australia, there are uncommon virtues and values.

What you find is in *your* hands.

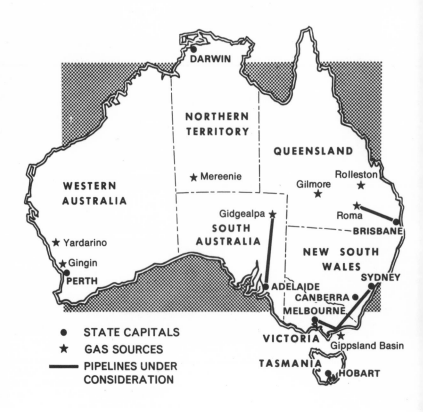

The golden, beckoning gateway to a city. . . . Princes Gate fountain, overlooking the Yarra River at Melbourne's Princes Bridge.

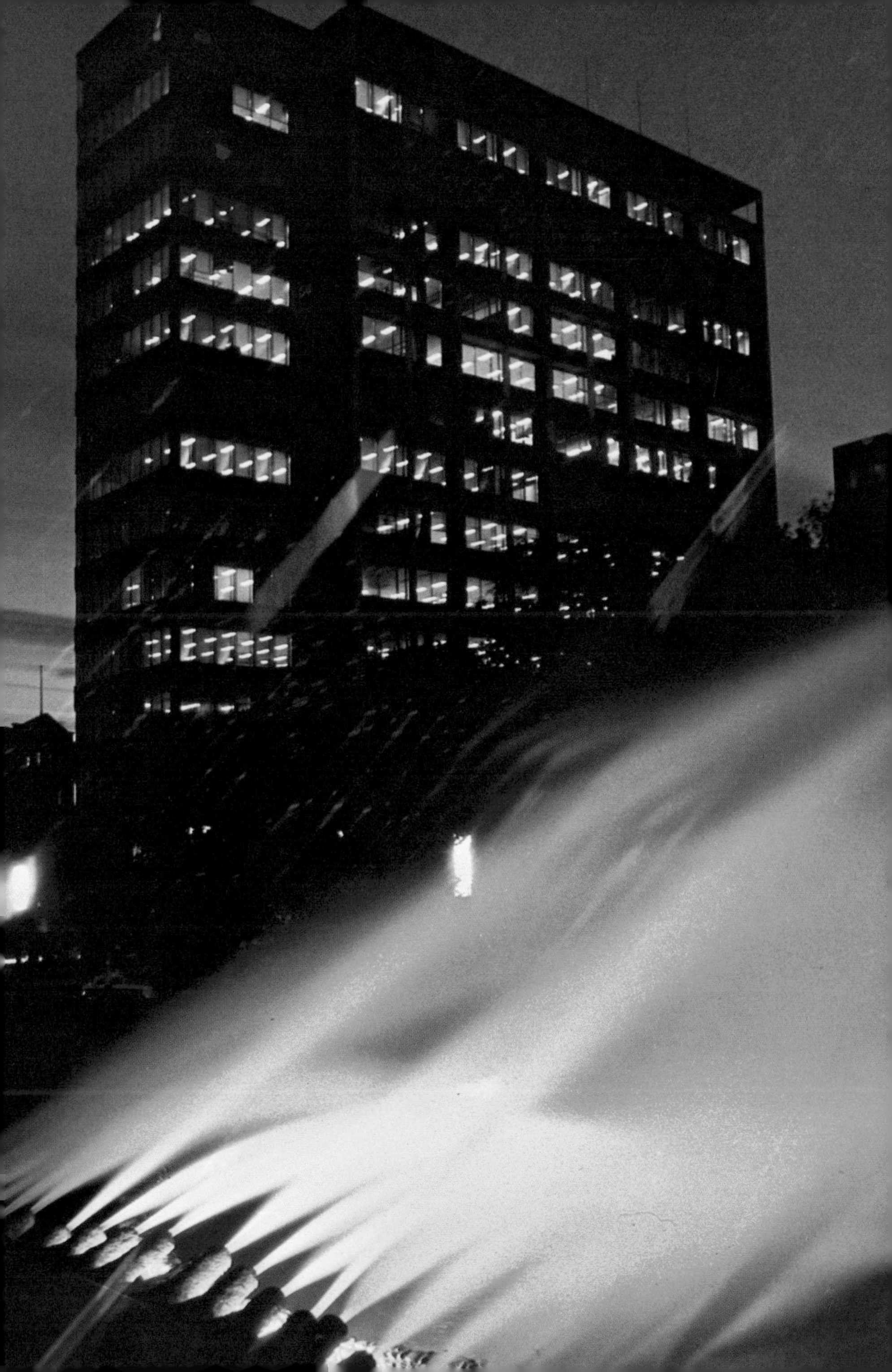

"... a barbecue from which he will produce excellent Sunday lunches, turn-and-turn about with his neighbour." T-bones, lamb chops, sausages, a beer, crisp salads, cheese, fruit, great wines, sunshine and 75-degree warmth; worth working for.

CHAPTER 3

THE PEOPLE

C ITIES EVERYWHERE are peopled by folk with heavy claims to the description "average". These folk have a safe, conforming personality; in some cities this safeness goes as far as making the individual part of the clump . . . an amorphous nothing, a cypher, a uniformity of mediocrity. But Australian urbanites tend the other way, toward an outgoing, airy type of adventuresomeness, based on *voluntary* conformity . . . yet still prospectful, unhidebound.

Indeed, Mr. Average of any Australian city is far removed from Mr. World average. He holds down a good job, at good pay; for which he returns a moderate to fair week's work. He eats very well indeed, dresses well without strictures, and arrives on the job on a summer morning in shirtsleeves, probably rolled. He works a forty-hour week at most, abhors and resents overtime . . . but very frequently does a part-time job to eke out his pay. If he chooses to get well ahead he'll have to do two full-time jobs, and a ninety-hour week.

He is paying off a tiled-roof brick veneered home, on a cheerful suburban block of land with a 60-foot frontage, 120-foot depth, and a grass "nature strip" between his front fence and the street. If he lives in Brisbane his house will be built on stilts for coolness or to exclude termites.

His backyard contains a lemon tree, an apple, a plum, a wattle, a couple of gums, a rotary clothes-hoist, and a barbecue from which he will produce excellent Sunday lunches, turn-and-turn-about with his neighbour.

His garage contains an Australian-built car, which he owns, a trailer, probably a motor-mower, and possibly a boat. He loves his wife, off-handedly on the surface but very deeply in the privacy of his home. Mostly she wears cotton dresses costing a few dollars, which she will keep very clean. In winter she wears slacks and a sweater. By conventional international standards she would qualify to be described as healthily sexy.

This suburban Australian's wife has borne him two children, one of whom goes to kindergarten and the elder to a state school. Education will cost him little, because they will almost certainly go straight to work from school without advanced academic training. They wear woollen uniforms in winter, cotton in summer, and learn to play ball games and to swim. They will certainly learn resuscitation, and probably how to treat snake-bite. Their educational standard will not be as high as it might, because of chronic school overcrowding.

Mr. Average and his wife shower daily, and in summer will probably shower in the morning, swim in the afternoon and shower again at night. They almost never bath. She is the world's greatest user of the contraceptive pill.

One of their in-laws almost certainly owns a "week-ender in the bush", or at the beach, where he and his family will spend four "long week-ends" during the year, and a fortnight at Christmas.

He loves six small beers "with the boys" immediately after work, and on winter Saturdays will probably shout himself hoarse at the football. During and after the game he will drink fourteen small beers, and become mildly and harmlessly tipsy. He fancies himself as the world's greatest beer drinker, which he is not. He also fancies that his beer is the world's best, which it is not. But it *is* inordinately alcoholic.

He seldom touches hard liquor, and reads very little, which is as well, because his literature is ferociously censored.

The world thinks of him as fiercely independent, but politicians and bureaucrats know him better as one of the meekest conformists, because he is civically bone-lazy, and has to be penalised for default to make him go out and vote. He in turn considers all politicians to be either stupid or crooked, which they are not, because they lead him by the nose, and by-and-large have led him fairly.

He is very slow to anger, and a smile comes more readily than a scowl. When angry, he is to be reckoned with. He is unsure of his origins, and doesn't much care about them, for few Australians

One in three of Australian wives goes to work to help eke out. Her husband thinks he has a forty-hour week, but if he hopes to get ahead he'd better do more; significantly more.

can trace their lineage farther back than Grandpa.

In summer he often "goes sick" to attend international cricket matches, which he watches with a handkerchief protecting his head, a beer-can in his hand . . . and unrancorous barracking badinage on his lips.

Most warm nights he sits outside with his family, and enjoys a couple of bottles of beer, contentment, and a hose-in-hand conversation with his neighbour. Most cool nights he sits inside and watches fiercely-censored television, or sees an occasional movie show, only slightly-less fiercely censored.

He gives up dancing at 21, except for an annual business ball, at which he gets mildly tipsy and exchanges mildly insolent banalities with his boss.

This Australian's house is well furnished, in moderate and extremely variable taste. He knows little of music or art, but he will often have a "Man in a Yellow Coat" or a likeness of a cheongsam-clad violet-lipped oriental girl on his wall as a concession to its existence.

A few years ago his taste in furnishings ran to uncut moquette, violent plywood veneers, skirted satin lampshades, flights of plaster ducks on the scumbled walls, and multi-colored Venetian blinds; but with the influences of Scandinavia this is improving fast.

If you are introduced to this Australian he will be prepared to like you, offer you the hospitality of his home, and be ingenuously interested in you . . . though wary. His conversation, though it may now carry overtones of a Sicilian mountain patois or Bavarian gutterals, will still be liberally sprinkled with the adjective "bloody". For some strange reason this unattractive word sounds hilarious when rendered in the accents of mittel-Europe or the Littoral.

Our average Aussie envies the upper-middles who annually winter in Queensland's Surfers Paradise sunshine, yet he knows that with any sort of luck he'll do the same within a decade.

A few years ago, on the occasions on which, much against his will, he was forced to eat out, he glumly ordered "steak and eggs", served unappetisingly, unappealingly and reluctantly by a scruffy

". . . a couple of bottles of beer, contentment, and a hose-in-hand conversation with his neighbour." **Suburbia, like any other Australian suburbia; from the Domain, Hobart.**

teenager in carpet slippers. Now he replenishes himself, with continental élan, at one of a superb array of bistros, taverns, brasseries and rathskellers.

Our city Australian is inclined to jeer at his country cousins in their wide hats, declaring them to be unendingly dissatisfied with the weather, and "always hunting for subsidies", an unconscionably large portion of which he feels will be tacked on to his personal tax bill.

All-in-all he is a "nice bloke", who pays his taxes, minds his business, and likes to be let alone when it pleases him.

His cities are growing spectacularly, in spite of anachronisms glaring to the international visitor.

Flyovers, cloverleafs and freeways have transformed access to his cities, but inept and unvigorous planning has stifled the hearts. Australians now shop in their neighbourhood supermarts, and visits to the "golden miles" are only essayed for the purposes of business, doctor's consultations, or for "an outing" . . . for no matter how stultified, the hearts of the cities remain the hearts, focal points of adventure.

However, flyovers and freeways help the cities empty fast and the mass exodus from any one of the eight Australian capitals on a hot Friday afternoon is a sight to stagger the senses.

Though retailing is going to the suburbs, cities will continue to burgeon, because big—really big—business is still transacted mainly in the capitals, and all the excitement of a growing nation is written clear on the "big boards" of the Stock Exchange; millions of Australians have a stake, large or small, in industry or pastorals or mining, and the plumber of today can well be the tycoon of tomorrow. "Funk money", too, pours in from other, less vigorous economies, as the old world scrabbles for a foot in the golden door of a growing continent's future.

All this concerns our Mr. Average Australian but little. He knows that policy is decided over fine Scotch and cigars in the leather deeps of the oak-panelled Georgian-facaded clubs . . . but this disturbs him not one whit.

He has his wife, his children, his car, his football team, his beer . . . and his faith. The sun pours down on his abundant health, and all's well with the world.

"*. . . the mass exodus from any one of the eight Australian capitals on a hot Friday afternoon is a sight to stagger the senses.*" A torrent of cars pours onto Sydney Harbour Bridge, headed to northern suburbs and beaches. There is no attempt to rationalise quitting times. Everybody pours away from work in a whirlpool of metal-on-metal, to an obbligato of shrieking rubber borne on the monoxide-laden fug.

Do you understand, then, why he *chooses* to conform?

He chooses thus because his happiness is perhaps more complete than that of any other Mr. Average on earth . . . although erosions are setting in, he is still all-but without fear!

But try to take all this away from him . . . and see him as he really is.

His strength is immense, his resolve unyielding, his courage unflinching and his dignity profound.

This Australian city-dweller, though he chooses to be led, is no sheep . . . he is a man of enormous stature, nice to know.

T O ACHIEVE the same result as his city-fellow, that of being a "nice bloke", the average Australian country-man follows an entirely different course.

His property might be a few acres of loam in the crook of a river's elbow, or it may be a shimmering, mirage-haunted vastness five times the size of a Balkan country.

He may run it with the help of a single addled lad from across the creek, and ride his boundaries on a placid grey . . . or he might run it with a payroll clerk and two accountants in an air-conditioned office, and ride his boundaries in a twin-engined Cessna.

Whatever the size or scope of a country-man's property he has one common denominator with his peers: all are engaged in a lifelong battle with the soil, for Australia has never yielded easily.

Picture the life of a no-more-than-average woolgrower, one of the tenders of Australia's 170 *million* sheep, about whom the city man will say, "he lies back on his veranda and watches the sheep grow fat".

His lambs are born about late autumn, and these huddled, defenceless, pathetic white fluffs will forthwith become the targets of crows, foxes, black frosts . . . and the ubiquitous dingoes, ultimate scourge, which, like slavering, satanic symbols of judgment, will decimate a flock for the unholy joy of killing.

The lambs will have to be tailed, castrated, drenched, marked and dipped.

When heavy-wooled they will face further unremitting assault of the kind that perhaps only Australia can wage.

". . . one of the tenders of Australia's 170 million sheep. . . ." **Dog and master round up newly-shorn flock in Victoria's Murray Valley, near Corryong.**

Blowflys will strike them, so terribly that the whole fleece will slough off on a carpet of seething maggots.

If drought strikes (and an Australian drought can last ten droning years) the sheep will have to be let die, for nobody wants stock in time of drought. This is the sheepman's only time of veranda-sitting: bitter leisure, to watch the grass shrivel and the land desiccate and blow away.

Or cataclysmic opposite, if flood comes . . . to drive the poor dumb flocks to higher ground, watch even that sanctuary engulfed and sit, benumbed and helpless, as grey bobble heads sink in turgid bough-filled scum.

Consider the most terrible of woolman's words . . . "bushfire".

Creeping, consuming groundfire, eating with slow inevitability at the margins of the land; grassfire, fast enough to run sheep down and pass, leaving blackened carrion . . . crow-mounted. Crownfire, ultimate holocaust, when the tops of centenarian trees shrivel, writhe, explode and roar, sucking value from the superheated air till a single searing breath means death. Ever see a giant tank into which a family has leapt, seeking succour, finding horror as the water boiled and made satanic soup, stirred with their poor stripped dead-pink bones? Australia has!

Consider weeks of unremitting rain, and face this thought: Ten thousand head, waterlogged, each fine sheep carrying in his fleece half his weight in rain. If he falls he will not, cannot, rise; he must be mauled and manhandled to his feet. To dry out, the mob must be taken on the road and walked; and for sixteen hours a day, for weeks of backrending agony, the sheepman must walk behind and hoist the fallen to their quavering feet.

Footrot? Carve till the blood runs sticky-slushy in your boots.

Crutching? Slash till you think the stench will never leave your throat.

Shearing? Bend your martyred back, hold your weight in stupid sheep between your knees; and in century heat ram a balky cutter through five-inch thick swathes of lanolin-laden wool for an eight-hour purgatory-day.

And will the city man help, or even understand?

No indeed; he'll smile at your wide-brimmed hat that thwarts

Drought! ". . . *bitter leisure, to watch the grass shrivel and the land desiccate and blow away.*" Sheep scratch in stubble field for scraps of nothing, with the sky an oven and rich loam turned to powder.

the summer's blazing sun or stops the winter's icy rain from soaking your prematurely-arthritic back. He'll tread your fences, shoot your lambs, pester your wife with price-inflated encyclopedias or shoddy Persian rugs. He'll fight subsidies and aid, yet live like a noble out of a wool-based economy.

The country man will tolerate the city man, even like him as an individual . . . but he'll be hard-pressed to collectively respect him.

Does this sheep man seem blunt?

He's not.

He's taciturn, honest, perceptive, resilient; and in his fashion, sensitive.

For though disaster's never far enough away he's also got the dreaming days; when the whole land flowers and basks in air that's virgin-sweet, the sky's a roof of God-brought wondrous warmth . . . and deepest peace abounds.

The dreaming days; faith fulfilled, ecstatic measure of reward for toil.

How lives this countryman?

His home, above all, is simple.

A vast kitchen with a slow-combustion stove that is lit when installed and whose ruddy heart is like a barometer of fate; high when happiness abounds, dully flickering when death is in the air . . . never extinguished till that Doomsday when it consumes itself.

A kitchen table of scrubbed bare boards; lean in drought, groaning at Christmas.

A coolgardie safe, lake-topped, towelled sides cool . . . housing inevitable grey-red mutton cuts.

Sack of sugar, sack of flour; tins of jam and kettle singing . . . picture calendar of sea.

Brass double bed, snowy cotton spread, marble-topped table, crouching wardrobe.

Matched gold-framed pictures on the wall; one of Grandpa, redolent in celluloid collar, alpaca coat and bristling jet moustache; one of Grandma, mellow-eyed, high collared, bustled, bunned and cuffed . . . they grubbed the trees and tilled this virgin soil.

"... *the dreaming days, when the whole land flowers and basks in air that's virgin-sweet; the sky's a roof of God-brought wondrous warmth ... and deepest peace abounds.*" Lambs and blossom in an elbow of Morse's Creek, near Bright, NE Victoria. Spring.

Home . . . more truly home than any city house!

These folk, the country folk, are close to earth; it's pungency a sweet awakening greeting.

Here the stars are close, the winds are personal . . . the seasons intimate.

Share this man's love of earth and he becomes your brother. Share his inept pause-filled thoughts and you'll be privy to values of a basic kind.

A "nice bloke" . . . genuine as soil.

These, then, are our two Aussies.

But most Australians will fail to see themselves here . . . for, after all, who in the whole world wants to think of himself as average; even if he is "*a nice bloke*" !

AUSTRALIA
AREAS OF PRODUCTION

Legend:
- 🌾 Wheat
- 🐑 Sheep/Wool
- 🍎 Fruit
- 🍷 Wine
- 🐂 Cattle
- 🐄 Dairying
- Prawns
- Crayfish
- Sugar
- Nickel
- Copper
- ▲ Coal
- ★ Oil/Gas
- ■ Lead/Zinc
-) Tin
- Mineral Sands
- ▲ Aluminium/Alumina/Bauxite
- Iron Ore

"*. . . the country folk are close to earth, its pungency a sweet awakening greeting.*" Children pick wild daffodils at Wandiligong, NE Victoria.

CHAPTER 4

THE HEARTLAND

"CENTRAL AUSTRALIA . . . The Red, Dead, Heart!"

How often has that worn phrase been uttered, painting its totally untrue picture of desert desolation, of waterless wilderness; of timeless, trackless nothing?

An untrue picture indeed, because Australia's heart, though certainly red, is very far from dead; and undoubtedly, no desert.

Alice Springs is in fact the hub of a 15,000 square-mile fantasyland of towering, marching peaks, azure-hazed; of lush waterholes often color-flecked with pastel-petalled water-lilies, and of drowsy, eucalypt-fringed, sandy watercourses, serenely keeping their secrets of deep, cool artesian streams.

This ten-million-acre heart of Australia is six mountain ranges; and a geological grab-bag of amphitheatres, monoliths, gorges, canyons, faults, tors, fissures and pounds . . . and thousand-foot blood-red rock-walls.

It is composed of quartzite and granite, pudding-stone and feldspar, conglomerate and sandstone; on which grow mulga and spinifex, corkwood and eucalypt, casuarina and paddy-melon, ironwood and acacia, palm and daisy.

Over this heart fly eagle and owl, falcon and crow, bat and budgerigar, pigeon and swallow, galah and kestrel, curlew and cockatiel; and on its surface live dingo and camel, brumby and fox, donkey and mountain-devil, goanna and gecko, euro and skink.

This heartland has soil that with water will produce knee-high cabbage, fist-sized tomatoes, huge oranges perfect in flavour and colour . . . and pagan Sturt Desert Pea blooms four inches long in clusters like muscatel grapes.

This heartland is surrounded by four great deserts, one of them the world's third largest after the Sahara and Libya . . . yet it sits

"This heartland is surrounded by four great deserts. . . ." **Gold fossicker and camel train in 120-degree shade of corkwood tree, on the northern rim of the Simpson Desert, about 130 miles east of Alice Springs.**

on a two-thousand-foot-high plateau, aloof, cooled by high winds that nightly show mercy from the infinite, arid heat that surrounds.

This heartland has probably the world's finest winter climate; drowsy, 80-degree daytime warmth; sharp, two-blanket cool by night, and always near-zero humidity.

No, Central Australia is no desert; it is a scenically and climatically unique Shangri-La!

Famed in popular literature, Alice Springs itself is a bustling, thriving community; a stepping-off place for the tens of thousands of tourists who see The Centre, a way-station for northbound traffic on the 1900-mile overland route from Adelaide to Darwin, and an oasis with big-city amenities for Territorians with business to transact or playing to do.

Towns have personalities, just as cities and people have, and the personality which is being developed by "The Alice" is warm and pleasant . . . good to come back to. Imagine the delight with which, in the 1870's, men returned to the little Alice Springs telegraph station after days in searing heat and dust, thirsty and exhausted from their struggle with the 2,230-mile northbound overland wire. That delight still exists today, for even in the jet age the traveller seldom loses sight of the fact that he is a thousand miles from a major city. He experiences a heartfelt friendliness, similar to that of the early pioneers, when after having been "*out*" on his travels, he sights the familiar landmarks of Alice Springs . . . landmarks named with the acute native sense of fun . . . *Billygoat Hill, Nannygoat Hill; and Heavitree Gap.*

"The Gap" must surely be one of the world's most fascinating arteries. Through this hundred-yard wide cleft in the mighty Macdonnells passes the very life-blood of Alice Springs. The South road, South rail, telephone and telegraph, power and water . . . all those nerve ends meet at the Gap, and feed and activate the town.

Alice Springs today is superficially sophisticated, with air-conditioned suites for touring internationals and executives, first-class cellars and cuisine, grassy plazas, and modern buildings and homes . . . but simmering just below the surface is the old frontier town from which The Alice has only lately emerged.

"... *probably the world's finest winter climate; drowsy, 80-degree daytime warmth....*" The western gateway to Ormiston Gorge, very near the geographical heart of Australia, about 75 miles west of Alice Springs.

On balmy spring Saturday nights wandering tent-shows play the town, with the brassy jangle of twangy guitars and yodelling cowgirls. Young-blooded Aboriginal stockmen in red shirts, tight blue jeans, long sideburns, hand-tooled boots and sombreros parade with their simpering girl-friends (like hen-birds, poorer plumaged than the male). The sidewalks are teeming. Giant Territorian police in khaki rig and wide-brimmed, immaculate hats genially oversee the proceedings (this same breed of men, hard-eyed, handled trained Russian "couriers" with consummate ease when they tried to remove defectees from Australian soil). The hotels serve cold beer in frosty glasses, and the night above the town's open-air theatre is rent with the tumult of blasting American six-guns and tumbling Red-Indians.

But on Sunday mornings peace returns and the good citizens of Alice Springs, augmented by tourists and out-of-towners, attend their churches in humble worship.

One of Australia's most remarkable churches is the John Flynn Memorial, an architectural delight full of mystery and symbolism, and a fitting memorial to the man who brought mercy, succour and unction to the people of Central Australia . . . Flynn of the Inland. The Flynn Church stands on a well-watered island lawn in the heart of Alice Springs, and frequently has congregations that overflow onto the green grass and sweetly sing the praise of God into the velvet-purple Central Australian night. People of many religions rejoice in the strong weld of Methodist, Presbyterian and Congregational churches that have formed the "United Church of North Australia", which preaches love from the pulpit of "The Flynn". What finer memorial could man want ? Unity, Love, Oneness . . . all the values dear to John Flynn.

With the growth of Alice Springs it is proper that suburbs should appear. These are as yet undefined, amorphous . . . but they ring Todd Street and the town proper.

"The Gap" is to the South. Aborigines make their home here. Many of them are amiable mendicants, although the possibility of a shanty-town development has been thwarted by the erection of much low-priced, comfortable, air-conditioned Government housing. The "East-side" is a comfortable, well-to-do satellite,

"Young-blooded Aboriginal stockmen. . . ." And fine stockmen indeed; who sit a horse as though they were part of it, and turn it out for work groomed like a Melbourne Cup starter; who can work a horse for months on end in drought, and still love it and respect it; and be respected in turn by both horse and station-owner. Branding at Angas Downs, between Alice Springs and Ayers Rock.

linked with the town proper by a causeway across the Todd
River and dotted with well-kept gardens of lush grass and tropical
blooms. Many East-side housewives and mothers seldom cross
the causeway, shop and live in their own "suburb".

At the "North-End" (never called the "Top-End", a term
reserved for the thousand-mile-away seat of Northern Territory
government, Darwin), industry in the shape of transport, earth-
moving and oil complexes clusters around the Alice Springs
railhead and marshalling yards. It is bedlam here, on nights that
"The Ghan" is made up for its early-morning departures
southbound. This modern diesel train with its mile-long string
of passenger coaches, freight trucks, and sedan-bearing flatcars,
is a far cry indeed from the old Afghan camel trains for which it
was named.

Outward for 250 miles, to East and West, flow the Macdonnell
ranges . . . cloven by the Tropic of Capricorn.

In the East the Macdonnells peter out in the upper edge of the
Simpson Desert. To the West, desert again, this time the
Gibson; but not until a hundred miles of big peaks have come and
gone. Some of these mountains claw toward 5,000 feet, and the
peaks of Sonder, Zeil, Razorback and Heughlin are familiar to
millions as the subject of Namatjira paintings. For this was
Namatjira country, where the Aboriginal artist used to take his
brushes and colours and a simple swag from the Lutheran
Mission, Hermannsburg, and "go walkabout", a solitary but
never lonely figure, recording forever the place he loved.

The good Lutherans of the 1870's established Hermannsburg
in the face of terrible privation and suffering.

Pastors Kempe and Schwarz, fresh from theological school in
Germany, set out from Adelaide to a point on the map of
Australia where nothing whatsoever was shown . . . no water, no
settlements, nothing. All they knew was that at this point,
between the Macdonnells and the Krichauffs, there were large
numbers of natives on the move, and therefore there had to be
water, of some sort!

The young pastors, high in heart, set out with an absurd
caravanserai of sheep, horses and cattle for a thousand-mile

"... for 250 miles, to East and West, flow the
Macdonnell Ranges, cloven by the Tropic of Capri-
corn." Fantasy of vertical strata near Glen Helen
Gorge, about 80 miles west of Alice Springs.

odyssey of Biblical suffering and testing. They struck North from the tiny hamlet of Bethany at the worst possible time, late October . . . direct into a terrible Central Australian summer, through country already fast in the grip of drought. Unrelenting, unremitting sun seared and desiccated the party. It must have seemed to the young pastors, straight from the cool valleys of their German fatherland, that the gates of Hell itself had opened to devour them. Packs of starving dingoes ravished their weakened flock in broad daylight. Wagons fell to pieces, and the little party straggled out to a sick, hungry, three-hundred-mile-long shambles. Only grit and faith were unflagging, exalting them through frightful privations to the end of a journey which has become an Australian epic. In June of 1877 the young pastors bared their heads beside a brackish waterhole scrabbled in the sands of the Finke, and gave thanks to God for bringing them to their promised land . . . the site of Hermannsburg. Their 3,000 sheep inevitably had shrunk to a handful, and their journey of hope had taken them nearly two years . . . but Hermannsburg existed!

Today the mission is the biggest and most flourishing in The Centre. Acres of gardens and some thousands of cattle burgeon, fed by water from bores, dams, and a five-mile pipeline from Kaporilja Springs. A modern school teaches hundreds of chubby Aboriginal children, for malnutrition has disappeared, and the birthrate is soaring.

Hermannsburg is the gateway to a number of The Centre's finest tourist resorts, among them Palm Valley, Glen Helen . . . and fabled, fabulous Ormiston Gorge.

Glen Helen is without question the most attractively-located tourist resort in Central Australia. It sits, elevated, a few hundred yards from the Gorge, whose permanent water must be negotiated by incoming tourists in (of all things) a tiny rowboat ferry.

From the homestead, a gentle slope of sand runs down to near-permanent water, fringed with cycads, the oldest palms on earth. Abruptly, a blood-red rock wall leaps 800 feet into the air. Winter here is enchantment. The wall faces the sun, soaking up its bounteous warmth all day, then releasing it against night's chill,

". . . gateway to The Centre's finest tourist resorts: Palm Valley, Glen Helen . . . and fabled, fabulous Ormiston Gorge." **Twin ghost gums by the roadside a few miles west of Alice Springs, on the Hermannsburg Mission road.**

reflecting downward on the little white resort homestead.

But the excitement of Glen Helen is not Glen Helen itself . . . it is the surrounding complex of natural wonders. Namatjira's special love, mauve-peaked Mount Sonder, is nearby; and Redbank Gorge and Mount Zeil; but these attractions, though startling, pale to nothing beside the cliché-named "*Jewel of the Centre*" . . . Ormiston Gorge.

Never was cliché more richly earned!

Ormiston is a red wall four-hundred feet high, reflecting the brilliance of red sun at an absolutely ideal forty-five degree angle into another red wall . . . this one a thousand feet high!

Walk for forty minutes along the sand-fringed permanent water in the gorge and you will use a couple of thirty-six exposure rolls of colour film and think you've captured Ormiston's magic. Start your walk back and you'll stop . . . thunderstruck. For the whole gorge has changed utterly. Plum, sapphire and emerald have replaced oranges, reds and burgundies. Even the air itself seems to have colour; and these colour changes go on hourly, infinitely variable, as Ormiston stages its daily chromatic floor-show, justifying its "jewel" title a thousand, then ten thousand times over.

The colour of Ormiston is more than a feast; it is a surfeit, literally an assault on the colour senses. A sunset in Ormiston alone or with another very close, is a shattering experience, whose vigor is all but beyond the power of human capacity to absorb and remember, for this is the very essence of Earth.

In their smaller way the scenic attractions to the East, on the run back to Alice Springs, augment the massive spectacle of Ormiston. Oddly, Serpentine Gorge, Ellery Creek Gorge, Simpson's Gap and Standley Chasm all have their own unique appeal; they are by no means anti-climactic.

Air-conditioned buses now make the eastward run from Glen Helen to Alice Springs, along roads that were camel-pads so very few years ago; and should you feel the need to get in touch with the outside world your driver will stop, light a fire, and, while the billy is boiling, radio your telegram for reception minutes later in Melbourne or Sydney or New York with the exciting "Office of Origin" legend, "*Alice Springs Outpost Radio*".

"_. . . Ormiston stages its daily chromatic floor-show. . . ._" Honeymooners at the western end of Ormiston Gorge. Colours change constantly, in infinite variety; a surfeit for the senses.

Pichi-Richi is an absolute "must", on the eastward run from The Alice.

Sculptor William Ricketts has brought his exciting ability as sculptor-Boswell of Australia's Aborigines to Alice Springs. Here, just outside Heavitree Gap, the Aranda-named "Kangaroo-rat Man" has created his sculptured masterpieces in a vandal-free oasis of peace. All the mystique of a mystique-ridden people is here to be seen, and even felt, tangible. The awesome "Tree of Life", the terrible "Bushfire Goddess", the benign "Moon Man" and the Kangaroo-rat self-portraits are important, stirring works.

Some fifty miles to the East, beyond Pichi-Richi, is Central Australia's most pleasant resort, Ross River.

Roomy cabins of rough natural timber, with floors of hand-cut local stone and individual showers and utilities, surround a grassy sun-trap, furnished with comfortable outdoor lounges. The old homestead, restored and enlarged but with its integrity intact, houses lantern-lit dining-rooms where excellent food is served on spotless napery. Just-right high-fidelity music filters from the dining rooms into the lounge, cosy with its deep leather chairs, library of things Australian, and open, huge fireplace.

Immense barbecue steaks from prime, carefully-selected Ross River beefs, and crisp home-grown salads individually boxed are aboard when the day trips from Ross River homestead leave for the old ghost-town, Arltunga. A thousand miners once lived here, in a brawling, bawdy community. Other day trips go to Trephina Gorge, to the "Valley of the Eagles", and to Ruby Canyon, where "not-quite" rubies may be plucked from the rock-dust of the canyon's floor, or gouged from its walls. Morning and afternoon stops are made to "boil the billy", and serve crisp, newly-baked biscuits, Devonshire Teas with feathery pumpkin scones, or light-as-air damper, cooked in an iron portable oven buried in hot ashes.

Ross River is traditionally a haven of relaxation. The lighting-plant is even located in a river-bed, a hill and a hollow away, so that the native peace may remain undisturbed.

It is always with reluctance that a Ross River guest will face the journey back to Alice Springs, but of such small reluctances is the

". . . *Central Australia's most pleasant resort, Ross River.*" Enjoy riding over untrodden earth; for a thrill ride go cross-country with an Aboriginal stockman, for a fun ride go on a placid grey with someone special. Riders near Bloomfields Bluff.

cloth of life woven, and the will to return to old friends maintained.

The future of The Centre is big . . . as big as the land itself. Tourists feel the hand of welcome, which is extended readily because Territorians understand well that their visitors are not boozy hedonists seeking pleasure, but discriminating, adult people with enquiry in their minds and adventure in their hearts. So tourism bulks large in the future of The Centre, as well it should.

But life in The Centre goes on, when the tourists have gone and summer grips the earth and powders it and sucks it dry.

Then for these months the universe of Centralian families revolves around two all-encompassing essentials . . . water and radio.

No journey will be undertaken without a ten-gallon can in the car, nor without some responsible person knowing that a car is on the move and is expected to arrive at a given time; for six hours away from a stalled car, without water and shade, can still kill, just as it could from the beginning of time.

But now, should a car fail to arrive within half-an-hour of its estimate, its driver at once has many friends, and the same air that shrills with cicada music is supersonically alive with radio'd plans for swift, sure help. This writer, bogged in a deceptive riverbed in 118 degree shade-heat has personally had the wondrous experience of seeing trucks arrive within the hour from both east and west with shovels, winches, and cold beer.

Although most of Central Australia is shown as being to the west of the Great Artesian Basin, its many rivers are said to run "upside down", and the watercourses are only rarely seen running. The Centre has a ten-inch rainfall, but this is infinitely variable from area to area. A flash downpour four or five miles away may be hidden from view by mountains, and strangers to this unusual procedure have been mildly amazed, then as quickly terrified, as a five-foot wall of water rips into view along a hundred-yard-wide dry, sandy riverbed, shimmering with heat under a cloudless sky. Such floods, as quickly as they appear are gone, and at first glance this seems a pitiful waste. Actually this coarse,

". . . summer grips the earth and powders it and sucks it dry." Or, worse, when seven consecutive summers desiccate millions of acres, till the only living things are seeds, cradled deep. After drought-breaking rain a Showy Groundsel, grim-fertilized, starts life anew.

extraordinarily porous riverbed sand is God's gift to The Centre, stowing and storing the precious liquid deep and secure from the sun. For although ten inches of rain falls annually, this bounty is subject to an evaporation rate of ten feet!

High-speed pumps bring back to the surface an abundance of water, sweet and clean and fit for any use. Ross River has a single pump, housed in its thirty-foot shaft, which can pump ten thousand gallons of water hourly, for days on end, without dropping the water table an inch. In Alice Springs a great series of pumps dotted along the kiln-dry sand of the Todd brings a permanent flow to replenish the thirsty reservoirs atop Billygoat Hill, supply the town's thousands, slake its gardens, and fill its swimming pools.

Radio is link, doctor, teacher and companion to the families of The Centre, and one of the real treats for visitors to The Alice is a morning visit to "School of the Air" headquarters, where tiny voices from hundreds of miles around recite haltingly but sweetly the verses of nursery rhymes to their air-borne school-mistress.

Flynn of the Inland's greatest work is perpetuated hourly, when the "Flying Doctor" comes on the air with spot diagnoses of radio'd symptoms, recommendations for alleviation of pain or illness from the coded contents of a basic comprehensive medicine chest; and even tender suggestions about an impending birth whose wonder can thus be vicariously shared with the entire outback. Should an emergency arise which a doctor feels merits personal attention, he invariably leans to the safe side and flies to give aid and succour. Modern aircraft of the Flying Doctor fleet are always on standby at The Alice.

A real treat for the strong, burden-bearing women of the outback Centre is the "gossip session", when an area two or three times the size of Britain becomes a radio round-table. Menfolk "out" mustering or bore-sinking a hundred miles from the homestead have trouble staying strong and silent when they hear the voices of loved ones; and these women, with ingenuous honesty, project in their broad and proud Australian voices a willingness to comfort their men, tenderly share their extremes of

Fifteen-hundred-million years ago, in the awful extremes of earth's birth-pains, a four-million-ton shard of conglomerate strata heaved its way, edge-on, out of Central Australia's miasmic ooze. Today, this shard, worn smooth, is the world's mightiest monolith, Ayers Rock. Enigma, challenge, photographer's feast, geologist's joy; it sits aloof and independent in a shallow basin of its own making on a flat, brown, spinifex-and-mulga-covered plain, just 220 air miles SW of Alice Springs, which in turn straddles the Tropic of Capricorn at Australia's heart. (But travel at least one way by coach; memorable.) The extraordinary brilliance of the Rock's displays is due to its ability to almost totally reflect low-angled light, while adding its own profound redness as an added bonus. Mica-like faceted feldspar generously plates the Rock's granite. The effect when these facets reflect already crimson dawn or sunset light is nigh unbelievable. Central Australia distilled.

(See also cover).

exhaustion . . . and keep the home secure for their return.

From November to April The Centre lives almost as it always has.

The Alice drowses in its rock frypan and the people of the outback fight their perpetual war against the savage land. Cattle, spreading a few to the square-mile, browse and doze in whatever shade they can find near the bore troughs. Shimmering mirage lines float dreaming purple hills in thick air, disturbed only by an odd skirmishing 'dust-devil.' The pace of all endeavour slows, and an after-lunch siesta is wisdom, not luxury.

The pattern for the future of The Centre seems well established. Aided by a vigorous and competent Animal Industry Branch, cattle, and the ability of the soil to feed them, will continue to flourish. Mining in the immediate Centre is now a ghost; although, Tennant Creek, to the North, is still prosperous, and much of its wealth channels through The Alice. But the true future gold of The Centre comes not from the ground . . . it comes from the May-to-October flood of pale-skinned, sun-seeking tourists. To this writer "tourists" doesn't imply camera-toting, overdressed loudmouths. These go to the big cities, and to glossy resorts whose contrived amusements are more to their tastes.

Visitors to The Centre want nothing more than to be a part of the beating heart of Australia . . . to feel the essence and mystique of this island continent. This feeling (because they live with it locked deep inside) Centralians understand and respect. They are good, plain folk; and like most such, inarticulate. But they love visitors because their pride in things Central Australian is fierce; and their need to communicate and share this pride is deep.

This is a giant land, where the hand of welcome is as big as the hearts of its people . . . and expended with an open, ready smile.

This is a land of the future; a proud, proud heartland . . . and, above all, no desert!

"*. . . the essence and mystique of this island continent.*" Ghost gum grows in solid rockface at Glen Helen Gorge, about 80 miles west of Alice Springs.

CHAPTER 5

THE 'TOP END'

I T IS ONLY a very few years since a visit to Australia's 'Top End', and more particularly, to Arnhem Land, was a 'tent, permit . . . and good luck' matter; but now, enlightened government policies, intelligent appreciation of the value of visitors to this growing country, and jet-borne accessibility have all combined to open up this most extraordinary corner of Australia beyond determined geographers to tourists seeking the unusual all-but-untouched corners of the world.

A journey to Arnhem Land will now probably start from Australia's most spectacular capital, Sydney, whose bustling $2\frac{3}{4}$ millions live at the east-coast hub of the Commonwealth. From Sydney the two domestic airlines run regular services to Darwin, and the 'Golden Boomerang' flight will carry you the 1,900-mile corner-to-corner journey between breakfast and afternoon-tea.

If you are sophisticated, making a cigarette commercial, rich, on an expense account, or in a hurry, you can jet Sydney-Darwin in a little over four hours; but you'll have to buy a ticket to Indonesia . . . Australia's domestic airlines agreement prohibits set-downs in Australia by international lines.

Darwin is the capital of the Northern Territory, whose area, six times that of Great Britain, is administered by Federal Government departments. This vastness, whose nature ranges from the most arid deserts to the lushest of rain-forests, is populated by less than a good football crowd . . . 20,000 Aborigines and 30,000 others.

Darwin itself is a multi-racial melting-pot, which reminds one perhaps of Honolulu. The community is a splendid working mixture of Aborigines, English-descent 'Old Australians', European 'New Australians', and Malays, Chinese, Japanese,

". . . this most extraordinary corner of Australia."
Cave paintings in the south face of Nourlangie escarpment, Arnhem Land.

Portuguese, Melanesians and Polynesians . . . all functioning together in harmony. The celebrated girls of Darwin are exquisite; exotic beauties in whose veins courses the blood of a grab-bag of cultures.

During wartime attacks, Darwin's heart was scarred by bombs, but new buildings and a profusion of flowers now cover the wounds.

The city is many paradoxes . . . its lifeblood and the income of a very big part of its population is government money siphoned from the taxpayers of southern States through the national capital, Canberra. But these taxpayers don't resent this particular expenditure; they realise that Darwin. is 2,000 miles from Canberra but only 400 miles from an intermittent source of sabre-rattling, Indonesia, 35 minutes' jet-flight away.

Darwin is a city without seasons . . . there are only 'The Wet', and 'The Dry'.

During the wet, from December to late February, the city's climate is enervating and relentless, humidly all-but-unbearable; inducing psychological depression-states whose unhappy by-product is the nation's highest per capita suicide rate. Even the relief of swimming is prohibited . . . the turgid Timor Sea teems with sea-wasps, venom-bearing jellyfish whose sting can paralyse with exquisite agony, then kill.

But the dry is superb.

While southern Australian States shiver their way through winter misery, Darwin enjoys 75–80 degree days, 75–degree ocean temperatures, and crisp low humidity . . . a winter climate for the gods. This supremely equable climate is one of the most valuable assets in the good-natured rivalry for tourist patronage that has broken out between the north and south of the Territory.

A tenuous, unnamed and unmarked border divides the areas. Below this mythical line the Northern Territory is known colloquially as Central Australia; shortened, it simply becomes 'The Centre.' Above the line the Territory is subject to a similar colloquialism; it has become Northern Australia, or 'The Top End.'

"The celebrated girls of Darwin are exquisite; exotic beauties. . . ." Chinese-Australian girl enjoys flower-scented warmth of a soft, tropic spring near Darwin.

The Centre, with its Alice Springs and complex of nearby resort hotels, its Ayers Rock, and its incredible topography, has long skimmed the tourism cream of the Territory, but now the Top End is hard on the Centre's heels, and Arnhem Land is perhaps the best inducement in this chase.

It is hard to realize, unless through our Australian eyes, how very important tourism is to Australia's north. It is deeply true, just here, to say of tourism, 'it's not the money, it's the principle that counts'. This enormous area simply *must* be peopled: to Australians, space-hungry Asia looms like an enveloping pall. Picture the vulnerability of the United States were only its western seaboard populated, and by a total population only slightly greater than that of New York City.

Bulking ahead of tourism as a people-attracting Northern Territory industry are only those incomes derived from cattle and gold, and at this moment cattlemen, as always, are fighting back at a country pitiless in its climatic vagaries. Some have seen no worthwhile rain for years.

Gold, too, is a tenuous basis for an economy.

Hopes were high for uranium a few years ago, but the value of the Territory's abundance of this atom-age fuel yo-yo's as atomic sophistications and requirements change.

Outside of Darwin all one's preconceptions of the Northern Territory are dispelled. For a hundred-mile radius a something-over-65-inch rainfall has created an astonishing complex of deltas, great ambling rivers, crocodile-populated swamps; and away from the coast, chain after chain of 'billabongs', permanent lakes of soft, clear water . . . sand and palm fringed like exotic tropic islands.

This billabong country is enchantment, and the safari tours that bring in visitors sell a real adventure in good Australian bush life.

Try such a tour.

After drinks in Darwin's air–conditioned Qantas terminal building, along with a jet-load of gritty travellers fresh from showering away the rime of Bangkok, you strap into the foam seats of a new, sophisticated-performance mini-airliner, and take

". . . an astonishing complex of deltas, great rambling rivers, crocodile-populated swamps. . . ." The Adelaide River, near Darwin, true rain-jungle; but very beautiful when a million water-lilies bloom beneath the drooping paper-barks and pandanus palms.

off from Darwin's immense city-long airstrip complex, which succoured American and Allied squadrons of World War II. To get off the paths of London-bound jets you make haste to set course due south-east, and sit back to enjoy a truly spectacular 50-minute flight to the safari camp airstrip.

Within minutes you sight your first herds of water-buffalo; great unpredictable brutes twice market-cattle size, wallowing in swamp mud, coating themselves thick with ooze to simultaneously soothe and prevent buffalo-fly bites.

Away from the coast the land loses its mangrove character and becomes classic Australian bush . . . a low-growing mallee scrub of eucalypts, slashed by patches of garish green where rainforest clamours for space along river courses.

Fifteen minutes out from Darwin a great, looping geographic fantasy grows before the nose of the aircraft . . . the Adelaide River. In places this extraordinary waterway, ambling in aimless fashion in search of the sea, loops through symmetrical three-mile arcs to within fifty yards of itself; and during one twenty-mile section of its seaward travel it is said to meander more than two hundred miles.

Thirty minutes out, and you can see your landfall, a fifty-mile escarpment, and dominating it, Nourlangie Rock, Australia's greatest gallery of primitive Aboriginal art.

With Nourlangie on the aircraft's nose you settle back to overfly one of the most astonishing wildlife aggregations on the Australian continent. You nose down to 150 feet, throttle back to slow cruise, and in this manner burst upon 'Goose Camp'.

The swampy lake's pearly surface foams and bursts to life as tens of thousands of wild geese dance their way along, rise, wheel and settle . . . for all the world like a vagrant cloud, a dense universe of feathered symmetry. Around the fringes, among the eucalypts and paperbarks, groups of buffalo lie, torpid and surfeited, idly watching the flapping confusion.

Now you can see the airstrip; a red gravel ribbon, fringed with billabongs, each with its spit of cleanest beach-sand.

You drift in to a friendly welcome, but the camp itself, at first glance to your simplicity-forgetting motel-critical eye, is a profound shock.

"... *a great, looping geographic fantasy grows before the nose of the aircraft*...." The meandering, crocodile-infested Adelaide River. About crocodiles: the up-to-25 foot Saltwater, which lives here, doesn't fuss swimmers (who are not overmuch to its taste). The up-to-10 foot Johnstoni is nimbler and more unpleasant, though skittery (and totally protected). If you feel like a swim, swim; but those prone to syncope should avoid treading submerged logs.

The kitchen-lounge is bark-roofed, open on one and two half-sides; and the cabins are bark-roofed, with the roofs suspended four feet above head-high walls of fire-palm stalks, with floors of puddled ant-bed, and with hand-made palm mats from the coastal Missions. But the beds are comfortable inner-springs, and the total effect at night, with yellow insect-repellent lights and huge mosquito-net bed canopies, is beguiling, bewitching, and very romantic. How soon one is able to forget the over-privacy of one's boxed-in, womb-like city environment!

The food is rough, would you think? Forget it . . . this is epicurean fare. Your evening meal will be buffalo-tail soup, followed with crisp deep-fried Barramundi (one of the world's really great gourmet fish) with an icy side-salad, and topped off with a platter of roast black duck that would make a Henry the Eighth banquet look like a kindergarten party.

The food is always superb; a couple of years ago this was a safari camp for hunters . . . but now the killing has all but stopped, except for food. The billabongs swarm with barramundi, who take a rubber frog lure and its hook like homing locomotives. Black duck and Whistle duck abound, and every week or two a choice buffalo is killed for beef.

Your rough old Australian cook looks after the supply of fresh food with the casual proficiency of one who has long mastered the fine science of making a hard land yield to him; while his Aboriginal lady, pipe clenched in her teeth, turns out fine light-as-air bread from flour with strange additives, baked in an ancient oven with a front like a chrome-plated tulip crop.

Your cook also has an attitude to his personal economic problems that has outraged many an ulcer-nursing tycoon obsessed with supertax persecutions, so simple and satisfactory is it to those concerned. He runs a beer, gasoline and tobacco account with the Chinese storekeeper at 150-mile-away Pine Creek, and when this amiable celestial passes word that his credit arrangements are becoming overstrained he simply takes his jeep and old army rifle to the billabong of his choice and shoots a crocodile. The Chinese storekeeper pays him $3.60 per inch of girth for the hide; and he finds that on this basis a

"The billabongs swarm with barramundi, who take a rubber frog lure and its hook like homing locomotives." Aboriginal guide's pup squabbles for possession of duck, which he feels is his due after hard morning replenishing larder.

16-footer yields him enough credit to keep him in little luxuries for a couple of months. This tough Australian, a bush-lover, shoots not for profit but to sustain himself at a tolerably reasonable comfort level.

If you plan to explore Nourlangie's trove of art in the morning you retire early, after some good talk over a bottle of Queensland rum, and rise with the sun. You join three fat Aboriginal children for a pre-breakfast swim in the billabong, demolish a buffalo steak washed down with black billy tea, hot and strong . . . with a tiny pet kangaroo joey nibbling absently at your bare toes.

Into the jeep goes twenty gallons of water, axe, pick and shovel, lunch; and a buffalo rifle in case you should accidentally flush an angry bull. Your host had been knocked out of his jeep and opened up very badly by an outlaw buffalo just a couple of seasons ago; lines of dull stitch-marks criss-crossing his body in random fashion remembered the occasion. He had been sewn up by an Aboriginal lady wielding a bag-needle, and the result is hardly invisible mending.

The jeep-ride to Nourlangie is a four-wheel-drive proposition, but well worth every bit of trouble. Repeated crossings of dry watercourses are made, and travel, possible only in the driest months of the year, is anything but dull. Frill-necked lizards scuttle, and when they feel cornered, turn and unfurl enormous neck frills, which make them appear ten times as large and twenty times as fierce, like a kind of executive panoply. The Aborigines call them 'blanket lizards', and find them delicious, lightly broiled.

All around there is life. Organ-grinder lizards perform their uproariously funny routine of running twelve or fifteen feet, standing high on their back legs, and working one front foot in circular motion, as though grinding a hand-organ. Stately five-foot brolgas dance dignified courtship rituals; then couple with enormously undignified erotic vigor, resembling nothing more nor less than a feathered whirlpool. Pairs of jabirus flirt archly in sandy creek-beds; and in every mud-wallow there are buffalo, ranging from calves as fat as butter to truck-sized monsters with seven-foot horn-spans.

". . . in every mud-wallow there are buffalo. . . ."
Group of water-buffalo (at water's edge, top right)
browse unconcernedly as a million Magpie geese
take the air. Goose Camp, near Arnhem Land's
Nourlangie.

Black cockatoos wing overhead, gossiping shatteringly as they go; and kangaroos fleet past, or placidly doze erect, their astonishing ears rotating through 300-degree sweep-arcs, alert against here non-existent danger.

There is an occasional tawny flash in the bush, far-off, as dingoes, those most-loathed of all Australian animals, like the wolves they resemble, slink their silent ways. Any Australian, born in a country whose income is predicated on the wool-clip, and having seen what a dingo will do to a hundred sheep overnight, would kill a dingo with his bare hands, given half a chance. Many Australians augment their incomes with dingo-scalp bounties, offered by State authorities.

You break from the bush-and-billabong country into an extraordinary area, which looks like nothing more nor less than a Scottish squire's game park. Lawn, nature-sown, sweeps away to the foot of Nourlangie, and on this lawn strut legions of wild geese and ducks, thousands strong. It is possible to drive the jeep at top speed in top gear on this surface, but the ducks and geese, totally unafraid, simply amble from your path.

Nourlangie is so accessible in the dry that one finds it hard to grasp that before the airstrips it was a chancy two weeks from Darwin to the escarpment.

The going is easy around Nourlangie's foot. Much of the rock's base is of quartz conglomerate, and as the softer material has weathered away the pebble-sized quartz chunks have dropped to form walkways of marble chips. The entire 50-mile escarpment is honeycombed with caves, fissures and gorges, and within the sheltering prominences, dreaming in the 85-degree warmth, there lies a revelation.

A millennium of Aboriginal art adorns the rock walls; art of many ages and many styles, a chronicle of Aboriginal needs, fears and gratifications. Here, too, is modern history in ochre; a ship sails one wall, but the ship is a barquentine in full sail; beside it there is a firearm . . . a muzzle-loading blunderbuss. From the mouths of sleeping-caves issue 'mimis', benevolent spirits designed to protect the occupants from possession in the night. Whole walls of honeymoon caves are covered with erotic paintings

". . . within the sheltering prominences, dreaming in 85-degree warmth, there lies a revelation." Nourlangie escarpment; eucalyptus and fragrant wild quinine trees curtain galleries of Aboriginal art, much never seen by contemporary man.

of coupling husbands and wives. 'X-ray'-type paintings show a crocodile with belly full of dingo and kangaroo. One frieze of paintings, perhaps the most beautiful, is painted layer-on-layer with strange beings whose arms intertwine below heads with great distinct haloes. An extraordinary fact of this frieze is its utter timelessness; the picture could have been painted a thousand years in the past . . . or a thousand years hence.

It is staggering, as you look, to think that this art treasure is now within seven hours of Sydney, within twenty hours of London, within twenty-four hours of the United States.

A morning pottering around Nourlangie will reveal a score of caves with paintings strong enough to photograph, while hundreds remain unexplored.

Some paintings have been weathered away by exposure, and many at eye level have been ruined by buffaloes, which saunter along scratching their itching fly-bites on the rock walls; but for as many that have deteriorated, there are more which are in excellent condition, often due to the restoration activities of Aborigines who go walkabout and who strengthen fading paintings with natural materials, applied with natural skill.

More than anywhere in Australia, at Nourlangie one experiences timelessness; a strange feeling, induced by ideal warmth, utter peace, and the presence of the living past; one feels watched, yet at ease. There are indeed many places in Australia where one feels at one with earth . . . and Nourlangie *is* such a place.

After the usual regretful farewells and half-hopeful promises to return, you fly back to Darwin, rested, fortified, affected . . . and pounds heavier.

As a finale to your Top End tour you can make an aerial exploration of the Arnhem Land coastal Missions, government controlled but church-administered. Scheduled airlines fly the Missions circuit around Arnhem Land twice weekly, and you take off shortly after dawn to make the one-day circuit. Most of the Arnhem Land Missions are pouring out an abundance of superb bark painting, now becoming a fashionable Australian export, and Millingimbi proves to be an admirable place to photograph bark art production.

". . . restoration activities of Aborigines who go walkabout. . . ." Aboriginal lad strengthens cave art with natural ochres; and all the loving care of a Louvre restorer working on a Rembrandt.

If your arrangements are made correctly, and well in advance, you will be met at Millingimbi airstrip (another World War II construction) by an intense and dedicated young Methodist missionary, and taken on a tour of the Mission's facilities, to an obligato of the sweetest natural voices you'll ever hear, the Aboriginal tots of the church school.

Most of the Aborigines are at work; the men fishing from dugout canoes, far out on the glazed horizon; the old women weaving mats and baskets . . . and the young women engaged in a hazardous operation that raises goose-pimples on the viewer. Bare from the waist, they gossip and giggle while they methodically range through the mangrove-tangled shoreline . . . seeking out giant, ferocious mud crabs . . . with their toes! How any of them have toes left is a wonder, because the giant plier-like crab claws could snap a broom handle with brittle ease. After capture the crabs have their claws tied, and are packed into old ammunition cases for air shipment to the mainland and final appearances on Territory dinner tables.

The Millingimbi bark artists sit around under trees on the foreshore, in little colonies of two or three, preparing their barks with a fixative derived from (of all things) wild orchid-root juice. More juice is mixed with natural ochres, and the finest of hand-made brushes are used to paint in painstaking strokes, away from the artist.

All the barks are individual, and here and there artists are developing unique styles.

The clan patriarch is a prolific artist. He sits a little aloof, while the butterball-fat children of his many wives come to visit him and bring him little gifts. A picture of fulfilled contentment, he lounges on an old army blanket in the warm breeze blowing off the Arafura Sea, with wives to bring him food and fill his pipe, and his bark paintings to keep him happily busy.

There has been some talk that the Aborigines are being exploited for their art, because of the outrageous prices asked for big barks in London, New York and Paris. This is patent nonsense . . . in actual fact income from bark paintings comes back to the Missions, is paid into trust accounts, and is used on

". . . seeking out giant, ferocious mud crabs. . . ." Aboriginal tot with prize. Crab will fetch good price from mainland gourmets; money will help maintain island mission, Millingimbi.

prudent schemes to benefit the entire burgeoning populations.

The Mission at Millingimbi now has a diesel trawler, con-structed in Brisbane; and while you notice that the naval architect's specifications for the trawler include modern fish-finding and handling equipment and full electronic instrumenta-tion, you will also notice that the tiny home on stilts in which the Mission director and his wife and family live is spartan, simple, and without even basic comforts.

If there *is* exploitation of native bark art, it is somewhere further along the involved chain that stretches from the Aborigines, painting under the Millingimbi trees, to indirectly lit niches in the walls of executive boardrooms.

Some of the barks *are* magnificent, great five foot by three paintings that tell stories of tropical cyclones overtaking dugout canoes, stories of days when the mud-crabs are many and fat, stories of days when the hunters run down many kangaroos, stories of times when the turtles come and lay eggs enough for a feast . . . and stories from the dreamtime of dark things that don't bear explanation. The artists move around the barks as they paint, so the stories unravel like circular links of frozen newsreel frames; in brush-drawn cinemascope and ochre'd, glorious orchidcolor.

All the fashionable popularity of Aboriginal bark art in the world's capitals, and all the hustling by chic interior designers seeking bark art for smart wall treatments concern the artists not one whit . . . they sit smoking their pipes and being waited-on by their wives on the Millingimbi seafront; and if they feel that things are catching up on them, why, they simply pack a swag, pick a wife to carry it, and 'go walkabout', living off the face of Arnhem Land for a couple of moons, or until they feel like ambling back.

One last thing; the Mission's enchanting postal address: Millingimbi Mission, Crocodile Islands, Arafura Sea, Arnhem Land, Northern Territory, Australia. They can use help.

Back in Darwin, one may meet Bas Wie, an Indonesian who made history in 1946 when, at the age of twelve, he stowed away in the wheel nacelle of a DC3 flying from Timor to Darwin,

". . . circular links of frozen newsreel frames; in brush-drawn Cinemascope. . . ." **Bark-painter Djawa, a tribal patriarch; artist, raconteur and bon-vivant; producing board-room art from a jam-tin, crushed ochres, orchid-juice and a home-made brush.**

suffered the hours-long journey flayed, burned and frozen . . . to fall more dead than alive on the Darwin airstrip as the DC3 rolled to a halt. He was taken into Darwin's Government House and looked after for five years by the then Administrator and his lady. Today he is a happy, healthy and prosperous Darwin family man.

Darwin teems with colorful frontier characters—uranium miners, pearling lugger crews, buffalo shooters, safari guides, gold smugglers, ladies of joy . . . the list is endless. Most of them drift on, at the urging of the Territory police, but some are native, like the movie-loving Aboriginal who greeted a downed Japanese airman during World War II with the astonishing ultimatum, 'Me allasame Oppalong Cassidy . . . you stickem up!''

History tells Australians that ours is an old, old land, but a young country. The circumstances of our discovery are unknown, and though the honor of this discovery is claimed by Portugal, France, Holland and Spain, these claims are all obscure, and certainly none of them goes back more than four and a half centuries. But Aboriginal legends, told in the haunting still of Arnhem Land nights, carry dim word-messages of great visitations from the exotic countries to the north; far, far back in the 'dreamtime.' These ancient legends tell that the spoils of these forays were great shipments of sweet-smelling logs, almost certainly camphorwood.

The cave-walls of Nourlangie record history through the eyes of the most ancient race on earth . . . perhaps a cool cave-mouth somewhere in the great escarpment frames a faded frieze of oriental junks, decks piled high with camphorwood.

Would *you* like to find that cave?

CHAPTER 6

THE SEA AROUND

E LEVEN THOUSAND miles of coastline surround the Australian island; eleven thousand miles of storm-torn granite tors, Dover-like limestone cliffs, Mississippi-like deltas, and eerie lapping inlets with a rise of tide of fifty feet.

This awesome stretch, more than the distance from Melbourne to London, is a defence-planner's nightmare; and a coast-lover's dream.

Like the land, the coast is a confusion of geological extremes; but the most awesome features are the beaches, ranging from shingly-sandy coves to blinding infinities a mile in depth.

Australians and beaches are synonymous; remember, four-fifths of all Australians dwell on the fringing rim, and every major capital is a port. A summer's day, nation-wide, finds millions of Australians gambolling, swimming or just plain lazing.

Off the continental shelf the ocean's floor drops inky black to the deeps; but there's an exception to this rule, it's very name enchantment . . . "The Great Barrier Reef", world wonder!

The reef starts below Capricorn's Heron Island, and ribbons its way northward, thirteen hundred miles, the distance from London to Moscow. In places the reef is intermittent, but twenty miles in span; in places it's so hard and flat that it resembles nothing more nor less than a great arrowing autobahn, along whose shimmering crown a score of army trucks could drive abreast. And yet (reflect on this) this great wall's source . . . a polyp; match-head-sized and soft as butter!

Distance on the reef, through nature's tricks, though tangible is a droll deception. This writer has seen a shell-hunter dropped on the reef to pursue his hobby, then has driven off in a high-speed cruiser. Two hours later, and many, many miles away, the shell-hunter was still visible . . . though inverted, shivering in silvery

". . . *eleven thousand miles of storm-torn granite tors and Dover-like limestone cliffs. . . .*" The Twelve Apostles, carved by the Southern Ocean, near Victoria's Port Campbell.

aspic, and thrice as large as life. Such tricks are commonplace . . . in a salt-spray laden, century-hot broth of air.

Perhaps the best way to understand the reef's magic is to experience the wonder of Heron Island, where the Great Barrier Reef is born; for Heron is the very essence of all your preconceptions of the reef.

Heron Island is beauty, mystery, tropical extravagance, natural wonder . . . and sun, sun, sun.

There are now a score or more of resorts calling themselves Barrier Reef Islands, pleasant places all, but they are not in fact Barrier Reef Islands. For the most part they are mainland islands, the pinnacles of a vast mountain range that once formed the easternmost spine of the Australian mainland. Now the valleys that were protected by these mountains have sunk under the inevitable onsets of time and ocean, and the hoop-pined peaks, running for hundreds of miles northwards along the Queensland coast, protected from capricious seas by the Barrier Reef proper, have become the island playgrounds with which Australians and the ever-growing host of tourists are familiar.

These islands are between ten and fifty miles from the mainland proper, and on the average are thirty miles or so inside the Barrier Reef. Of all the resorts, Hayman Island can boast about the closest relationship to the reef . . . a scant fifteen miles. But an odd sidelight to reef tourism is that hundreds of thousands of tourists have come to these islands, had the honeymoon or holiday of their lives . . . but have come nowhere towards achieving contact with the reef proper. The wonders of the incredible marine garden have been denied them by the vagaries of wind, time and tide; for Barrier Reef navigation is indisputably among the world's trickiest. Even dour British Admiralty charts boggle, and the footnotes "navigation should not be attempted without local knowledge" show up time and time again among their cabalistic notations.

Little wonder that many scheduled trips from mainland islands to the outer reef are cancelled, or abandoned en route.

Happily, Heron's position negates these scrabbling reef forays; for Heron Island is *part* of the "Great Barrier Reef".

"*. . . Hayman Island . . . the honeymoon or holiday of your life. . . .*" **Prettiest and best served of all the Barrier Reef (Whitsunday) Islands, Hayman has a fine hotel and year-round tranquillity. Outer Barrier is only 15 miles east.**

The southernmost resort island of the entire chain, Heron is a true coral cay; a tiny, richly-wooded emerald diadem, formed by a myriad galaxies of coral polyps through dreamless eons of time. Now its trees are tall, its skirting coral sands of blinding, sun-drenched white giving way to waters of uncanny clarity . . . the warm broth of life for the corals, whose burgeoning life goes on in perpetuity.

But Heron's great attraction is the wonder of its natural advantages. At night the island and its waters creep and loft and surge and burrow with life, all of it fascinating, none of it inimical to man. Giant turtles sigh their centuries-old paths up the beaches, their sorrowful eyes brimming with wisdom. Each turtle knows deep in her secret heart that only a handful of the two hundred-odd babies that will thrust from her ten-week-old eggs will survive the terrible gauntlet from sun-warmed sand-nest above the tide-line to moderate security in reef coral . . . a gauntlet of hungry sea-birds, ambushing crabs and voracious killer fish. The turtle will shed real tears while laying; tears of affection for her unborn doomed young; tears of terror for men who once canned turtle flesh in a reeking, steaming Heron Island factory . . . and tears of fright for tourists who rope her flippers, squat fat behinds on her back and posture for cameras.

While the turtles invade the beaches, from November to January, Heron plays host to another fantastic migration. In the third week of October the sheerwaters come soaring to the terminus of their 8,000-mile southward migration. These birds have come winging from the tundras of Northern Siberia and the Aleutians. Their eyes have beheld Fujiyama, the Philippines, and the trackless, formless, glaring Pacific wastes. Unerringly they have returned to Heron, instinct-driven to the very burrows in which they first found life. With clumsy webbed feet sagging from tucked-up, unexercised legs, they fly with heart-rending expenditure of their last remote reserves of energy to heavy crash landings on Heron's beaches and cabin roofs. They lie stunned, immobile, all-spent . . . until the morning suns warm them, and restore the will to live. Thousands of sheerwaters perpetuate themselves on Heron, their soft keening and cooing wafting on

"... a true coral cay; a tiny, richly wooded emerald diadem...." Heron and its fringing reef. Hotel is at bottom left of island. Ship was sunk as breakwater to facilitate landings.

the night, competing with the usurped cries of the native bird inhabitants, noddy terns and herons.

But the greater wonders lie below . . . in the Pacific's translucence. Here the living reef awaits . . . the silent, uninvaded unspoilt world.

The exploring glass-bottomed boats are excitement in themselves . . . here where every detail of the coral kingdom's floor is intimately visible, though sixty feet straight down.

For a greater sense of reef-belonging, there's snorkelling . . . lazing along in the seventy-degree surface water, suspended in the sky of the underwater world; banking and turning, weightless . . . diving as the mood strikes one into the crowding clouds of prismatically-flashing fish.

For the supreme thrill of a lifetime . . . a dive with breathing equipment into the great reef's secret fastnesses. Only a tinge of nervousness disturbs this promise of sheer enchantment, when, with all equipment checked and working, you fall backwards over boat's side into twenty feet of balmy water. There is no discomfort, and after the flurry of your entrance settles, nothing to distract you from the incredible grace and beauty you behold, wide-eyed.

All around is a living, bustling, vigorous world, peopled with gemlike aqueous strollers. Its eddying highways are clearly defined, wending their way through storied streets of coral skyscrapers. Demoiselles dance their skittering solos, pompous Moses Perches transact their grave commerce, an octopus sneaks a tentative tentacle across a burgundy coral. His tentacle is burgundy, but his body the sand-green of its sheltering rock.

An amiable school of yellowtail come to have a look at you, and what a school; hundreds of fifteen-pound beauties. They make three slashing circuits, a few feet from your eager eyes, then make off, their fishy curiosity satisfied.

The game fish here are splendid . . . anglers' dreams, and in goggling abundance: even their names are magic; red emperor, sweetlip, marlin, coral trout, coral cod, groper; an occasional flash from a mackerel missile, shafting through a coral arch.

As you swim, you slip through coral crenellations of fantastic shape, for a further small miracle of the coral polyp's being is the

". . . *the living reef awaits: the silent, uninvaded, unspoilt world.*" Scuba-diver and friend; a fat, curious, bejewelled dowager coral cod. Flare helps him navigate caverns.

predetermined shape of the calcareous sky-scraper that will be born out of his million skeletal shrouds. Forests of stag-coral, flying-saucers of table coral, choruses of organ-pipe coral and fanning blood-red Gorgonia treelets . . . all abound. You admire a feathery, soft coral, and idly run your hand through it. It stings like a thousand nettles, defensively, then resumes it's wavering dance.

Still slowly, you swim over a sandy patch, a sort of pool within the ocean, and you realise with a start as you drift down that the entire pool's floor is carpeted with baby stingrays, harmlessly at play like sandy aqueous birds.

The light is soft, and blue-green golden . . . cathedral-like through coral naves and vaults.

All is beauty, all is silence, all is life . . . a dreamlike fantasy of softest hue, beggaring description, ultimately unforgettable . . . fitting climax to the story of Australia!

"*. . . ultimately unforgettable. . . .*" Hayman Island honeymooners explore the outer Barrier Reef, in a low-tide sunset; making memories they will treasure to the twilight of the new life just begun.

"... *kangaroos, kookaburras and bellbirds* ...
*wholly admirable little furred and feathered
creatures....*" White kangaroo scraps with friend in
hills near Adelaide. Albinos are surprisingly
common; there is even an island of them in the
Australian Alps' Lake Eucumbene.

CHAPTER 7

AUSTRALIAN 'GOODS AND BADS'

H ERE IS a list of things Australian . . . good and bad. It is a collection compiled by one person, who loves Australia with a quiet yet fiercely-cherished passion; and the very depth of this passion is a measure of intolerance for things thought imperfect.

Yet notice two things . . . firstly, the 'goods' far outnumber the 'bads' and, secondly, the good things are really great, while the bad things are, at worst, mediocrities.

The list acknowledges many very basic things, so it will almost certainly be dubbed naive. Why, the nod is even given to koalas, kangaroos, kookaburras and bellbirds . . . wholly admirable little furred and feathered creatures thought un-chic to mention in sophisticated ('Tell 'em about the big cities, mate') urban Australia. For this kind of thinking . . . a loud jackass laugh.

One must certainly present such a list with mixed feelings, but those of trepidation are outweighed by a pure fact of significant magnitude . . . in Australia one may say what one thinks, and even though the penalty may be sectional opprobrium, this will be of a degree and nature easily supported by a pair of broad Australian shoulders.

Herewith, then, with compliments and without apologies, *AUSTRALIAN GOODS AND BADS.*

AUSTRALIAN 'GOODS'

Bouganvillea on Queensland verandahs.
Kookaburras laughing, anytime.
Mud crabs at a Gladstone, Queensland, Greek cafe.
Moonrise on the Gibson Desert.
Grilled Red Emperor at the Restaurant Nautilus, Port Douglas.

Bellbirds in a fern gully.

Deep-sea fishing off Port Lincoln, or Cairns.

The Australian Ballet company, doing Helpmann originals.

Start of the Sydney-Hobart yacht race.

A Queensland fruit shop.

Pony-riding with Aboriginal stockmen.

Steak sandwich with damper and billy tea, Angas Downs.

Crayfish tails broiled over an open fire.

The Flinders Ranges, at wildflower time.

Sydney girls, doing anything.

Hobart and Adelaide Art Galleries.

Outdoor concerts, Melbourne's Myer Music Bowl.

Homestead garden at Atnarpa, Simpson Desert.

Waterskiing, at dawn, on the Gippsland Lakes.

Waterskiing, in the morning, Nerang River, Surfers Paradise.

Waterskiing, mid-afternoon, Lake Eacham, near Cairns.

Waterskiing, at twilight, Port Phillip Bay.

Any waterhole after a dust-storm, Central Australia.

Jazz in Rocco's Cellar, Sydney's King's Cross.

The park musician with his birds, King's Cross.

Apple blossom time at Port Huon, near Hobart.

'Free Speech' forum, Melbourne's Yarra Bank, Sundays.

The Victorian Alps in spring.

Hal Porter's writing.

A ferry ride to Sydney Harbour's Goat Island and Balmain, or Manly.

Scuba-diving, Wistari Reef, off Queensland's Gladstone.

Camel bells in the desert, at night.

Driving in Perth.

Sunday picnic, on a cruiser, Sydney Harbour.

Autumn at Wandiligong, north-east Victoria.

Kenneth Slessor's poetry.

Melbourne's climate in late spring and early autumn.

Darwin's climate in winter.

Hobart's climate in summer.

A slight breakdown in community apathy.

Frostbite Regatta on Melbourne's Yarra.

Wedge-tailed eagles flying.

"The Flinders Ranges, at wildflower time." **A hill is drowned in red wild hops, blue Salvation Jane and yellow daisies. Ranges start a few miles NE of Adelaide, spear north for 200 desert-fringed miles.**

Outdoor Shakespeare, Adelaide Festival.
Australian National University, Canberra.
Well-hung buffalo steak, char-grilled . . . and buffalo-tail soup.
Hawkesbury River holidays, on a chartered cruiser.
Some Australian art.
Flying a light aircraft, Australian Alps; or the Krichauff Ranges, Northern Territory.
The Murray Valley.
Racing at Melbourne's Flemington.
Woy-Woy.
Divine Service, Flynn Memorial Church, Alice Springs.
Ocean liners leaving Melbourne.
Ocean liners arriving, Melbourne.
Kangaroos browsing.
Koalas sleeping.
Ray Taylor and Max Harris, iconoclasts.
Pies.
Barry Humphries' writing.
Cheese.
Patrick White's writing.
Outback people at picnic races.
Outback people at any other time.
Tanner cartoons.
New Guinea coffee.
Test cricket on the Adelaide oval.
Hunter Valley red wines.
Melbourne football, Collingwood versus Carlton.
Working sheepdogs.
Barossa Valley white wines, especially late pickings.
Darwin's hothouse beauties.
Budgerigars in flight.
Fresh Avocados, Custard Apples and Passion Fruit.
Egalitarianism.
18-footers sailing in Sydney 'southerly buster.'
Keith Dunstan's column in Melbourne 'Sun'.
Tsindos' steak, Melbourne's Florentino Bistro.
Perhaps uninspired, but certainly stable government.

A furry mittful of gum leaves, a branch to doze on; if ever a creature didn't ask much from life it's the koala. And what he gives in return! He's the most lovable, dopey, cuddlesome creature on earth.

AUSTRALIAN 'BADS'

Overnighting in country pubs.
Australian censorship (bad).
Victorian censorship (worst on earth).
Much Australian art.
Many motel breakfasts.
Inarticulate sports stars.
State chauvinism.
Metropolitan parochialism.
'Top 400' sycophantism.
Mediocrity of local television, excluding documentaries.
Political apathy of voters.
Posture of chill-affected Melbourne girls.
High hidden taxation.
Melbourne driving.
Melbourne's sunshine average.
Adelaide, Perth and Brisbane tap-water.
Car servicing, anywhere.
Education; primary, secondary and tertiary.
Teeth.
Hotel food, with dramatically few exceptions.
Rude postal employees, excepting the few.
Strangled cities, excluding Perth.
Music programs on commercial radio.
Finding one's way into, or out of, Brisbane, by road.
Export of kangaroo meat.
Company crashes, and idiot figurehead directors.
Overgovernment; Federal, State, City and Municipal.
Bureaucratic authoritarianism.
'The Establishment', anywhere.
Vandals and litter-strewers.
Egalitarianism.
Bureaucratic contempt for the value of people's time.
'Soup, Boiled Mutton and 2 Veg., and Jelly and Trifle' menus.
'Wirescapes', and the clods who plan them.
A hopelessly inept postal service.

Australians still find themselves able to drop this delightful creature with a bullet-shattered shoulder, club out its brains, and export its meat for the delight of Californian dogs. This is the worst single thing they do. Kangaroos are becoming sparse. They could vanish.

NOTES

NOTES

NOTES

NOTES

NOTES

NOTES

NOTES